THE ROYAL FAMILY TODAY

This edition published 1984 by Book Club Associates
by arrangement with Colour Library Books Ltd.
© 1984 Illustrations: Keystone Press Agency, London.
© 1984 Text: Colour Library Books Ltd., Guildford, Surrey, England.
Display and text filmsetting by Acesetters Ltd., Richmond, Surrey, England.
Printed and bound in Barcelona, Spain.
ISBN 0 86283 127 X

D.L.B.34297-83

THE ROYAL FAMILY TODAY

FOREWORD BY
THE EARL OF LICHFIELD

TEXT BY
TREVOR HALL

PRODUCED BY
TED SMART & DAVID GIBBON

BOOK CLUB ASSOCIATES
LONDON

The Queen and the Royal Family are many things to many people, but they have always enjoyed a double appeal at least. Their subjects regard them first and foremost as a family – close-knit yet at times far-flung, special yet somehow typical. As far as their relationship with the people of Britain and the Commonwealth is concerned, they regard themselves primarily as a firm, an organisation bound by convention to acquit a lifetime of public duties as the inheritors of one of the most ancient and envied unwritten constitutions in the world. There is a dilemma in this dual identity, which perhaps the Royal Family appreciates better than its subjects – that of balancing inevitable or desirable publicity with the necessity of family privacy; of projecting a public purpose without destroying personal integrity or invading the intimacies of domestic life.

It is no casual misuse of words to say that during the first thirty-two years of her reign the Queen has successfully managed the solution. She and Prince Philip have brought up their children in such unspoiled privacy that their eventual public lives have developed and can develop to maturity and fulfilment, unharmed by over-exposure to the ever eager public gaze. Prince Charles is the obvious example of the accomplished fact: his sympathetic and versatile character drew him irresistibly towards his future subjects even before his impeccable choice of a wife endowed the monarchy with an unexpectedly priceless asset. Matchless for her storming popularity, the Princess of Wales seems already to have exercised an influence on her in-laws by showing how a closer rapport with the public can be achieved without conceding dignity or charisma. On a more personal level, the birth of her son, and the way she has combined motherhood with public duty have endeared her to millions, and in this respect Britain is the envy of the world.

Though the monarchy's prime functions are accomplished through its major personalities, it continues to depend heavily upon those less senior members whose roles are essentially supportive. Its greatest expert, Queen Elizabeth the Queen Mother, is also its pivot, fulfilling her duties in her eighty-fourth year with ease, charm and a sense of fun. Princess Anne and Princess Margaret have also shared a continuous round of public engagements, and will continue to do so until perhaps Prince Andrew and Prince Edward become available in their own right. Meanwhile the more junior branches – the Gloucesters, Kents and Ogilvys – maintain diaries of engagements in keeping with their many patronages, presidencies and personal interests.

In any one year, of course, the Royal Family's moments of leisure are sometimes as public as their official duties. In allowing this to be so, they illustrate how we may legitimately look upon them as a family typical of any other, provided we understand and appreciate the other, more serious, sometimes rather oppressive side of their existence. It reminds us that though our vision of them as a family is valid, the institution of monarchy flourishes only because of the dedication of its individual members acting as an efficient and hard-working team.

RT. HON. THE EARL OF LICHFIELD F.I.I.P., F.R.P.S.

Shortly after midday every Christmas morning the huge, ornate doors of St George's Chapel Windsor are swung open. A twinkling of lamps and candles breaks the gloom within and the surging sound of organ music drifts out, evaporating into the crisp December air. For a while that scene is frozen, except for the few, dark-suited officials who dart around outside, nodding and winking to warn others of impending activity which seems slow to materialise. Then a cluster of clergy gathers silently at the doorway, serenely awaiting the duty which is that of every parish priest – to greet and bid farewell to a departing flock.

On this occasion, the flock is no ordinary one. No less a personage than Her Majesty the Queen leads the informal procession of exiting worshippers, stopping for a brief word of Christmas greeting with the Dean of Windsor and his assisting clerics. A step or two behind her – after nearly forty years of marriage he is irreversibly programmed into the habit of conceding precedence to his wife – Prince Philip searches out the army of press photographers ranged along the Castle ramparts. Their cameras shoot back as he exchanges a few impromptu comments – some looking humorous enough from a distance to suggest gentle irreverence – with his ecclesiastical hosts. Together, and perhaps accompanied by one of these magnificently robed churchmen, the Queen and her husband walk slowly and casually down the Chapel's wide grey-stone steps, eyes directed sometimes at each other, sometimes to the spot below where their cars will arrive to take them back to the Castle's private apartments, sometimes back up the steps as if waiting to be joined by relatives of lesser precedence.

They are neither far behind nor, these days, small in number. Headed by the Queen's own children – all of them adult, since the youngest, Prince Edward, now verges on his twentieth birthday – the contingent includes her mother Queen Elizabeth, her sister Princess Margaret, her in-laws, like the Princess of Wales and Captain Mark Phillips, cousins in the shape of princes, princesses, dukes and duchesses from the Gloucester and Kent families, and the Queen's only surviving royal aunt, Princess Alice. The order of family (and for that matter State) precedence is strictly observed, though eventually broken by the comparatively disorderly ranks of young children, from Master Peter Phillips to Lord Frederick Windsor, who begin to hop and skip about, pulling their parents out of line with them as the family gathering widens out from the restricting doorway to take full advantage of the expansive steps. Eventually, small groups begin to form: Princess Margaret's children will chat to their Kent and Ogilvy cousins; the Duke and Duchess of Gloucester with Prince and Princess Michael; and Princess Alice may choose to catch up with the Queen Mother. Eventually, a succession of black limousines arrives to ferry each family unit back to what they endearingly call home.

Unless the first of these is unusually prompt, those august steps will, for a brief space of time, bear almost the full complement of today's Royal Family: a veritable staircase of royals. A few absences are inevitable: a brief indisposition, a sojourn abroad, or the fact that infants do not make suitable churchgoers means that the royal Christmas morning gathering is never quite complete. But that one minute – it will rarely be longer – provides the only opportunity from one year's end to the next for the public to see, through the lens of the press camera, such a comprehensive assembly of Britain's first family.

It is tempting to suppose that the Queen wishes it this way as an expression, for all the world to appreciate, of the domestic unity by which her family has been popularly and persistently characterised. The combination of that fleeting corporate pause and the tolerated presence of the British press within those revered castle walls seems to operate as one of the Queen's tactful and dignified concessions not only to public curiosity, but also to the necessity of proclaiming from time to time the closeness of a family which for much of the year is continually on the move. To that extent, the concession certainly achieves its purpose.

It also vividly reminds us how much the Royal Family has grown in the last twenty years. Quite where it ends is difficult to say, since parts of it which we tend to class as royal – notably the children of Princess Anne, Princess Margaret and Princess Alexandra – are not strictly royal at all.

But by any account, the annual Christmas reunion at Windsor is certainly the biggest that could have been mustered since the days of Edward VII. He, by reason of his eight brothers and sisters alone, could virtually have filled Windsor Castle with nephews and nieces to two or more generations.

Indeed, it was the growing size of the Queen's family which prompted her in the mid-1960s to abandon Sandringham as the customary venue of her Christmas festivities in favour of the more numerous and spacious rooms of Windsor Castle. Before the weddings of Princess Margaret in 1960, the Duke of Kent in 1961 and Princess Alexandra in 1963, there were fewer than a dozen adults and barely half as many children to cater for. Now the company comprises almost three dozen relatives – all representatives in one generation or another of the children of the Queen's grandfather, King George V. Only the Harewoods – the family of the late Princess Royal – and the desolate, senile Duchess of Windsor, now in her 88th year, take no part in the Windsor celebrations. Their absences are attributable, in varying degrees, to the effects of divorce in a less tolerant age, and to the inevitable drift, even in the most royal of circles, of the more outlying members from the core of the family unit.

It seems to be common ground that the Royal Family has a whale of a time at Christmas, though only the fly on the wall – if such creatures are tolerated at Windsor Castle – is privy to what really goes on there. The dinners and parties, all on a grand scale yet preserving the essential family atmosphere, are more than mere celebration. Like most of her subjects, the Queen feels that she and her relatives have deserved those few brief days together – a respite, a reunion, a polite merrymaking after a year of intense activity, unremitting publicity, triumph and difficulty, brickbats and acclamation.

The Royal Christmas is just one of many focal points which shape the Royal Family's year. Some of those focal points are occasions of duty, like Trooping the Colour, the Remembrance ceremonies, Commonwealth Day observance and the Maundy Service – a pattern of almost unchanging ceremonial staged, generally speaking, at fixed times of the year. Others are interludes of private leisure which through long-established personal traditions have become as public – or more so – and as expected as any State Opening of Parliament: Badminton Horse Trials in April, Royal Ascot in June, Cowes Week in August, and the Braemar Gathering in September.

Within that year of major occasions are weeks or months when the royal pattern seems equally repetitive. For the Queen, there are up to a dozen major investitures each year, mostly geared to the spring and autumn months; summer witnesses a rash of garden parties at Buckingham Palace and Holyroodhouse. Almost every week the Queen spends in Britain is punctuated by numerous audiences with world diplomats, new public appointees and, most significantly, by an early – usually Tuesday – evening conclave with the Prime Minister. For Prince Philip and the Prince of Wales, there are endless waiting lists of meetings to be chaired or presided over. Princess Anne's commitment to the Save the Children Fund and Riding for the Disabled account for anything up to three dozen of her annual engagements. All members of the Royal Family must give periodic audiences to incoming and outgoing officers and officials of the scores of organisations – from regiments and other service units to charitable institutions and committees – to which they lend their patronage. For all of them, from the Queen downwards, the faintest hint of boredom in a repetitious schedule is to be avoided. Every visitor, however frequent or however insignificant, to the royal presence must be made as welcome as if the occasion is an unrepeatable novelty for both parties. It was once said of Queen Elizabeth the Queen Mother that she has the astonishing gift of being sincerely interested in dull people and dull occasions, and of making each individual feel that it is to him that she has devoted that lovely smile. That is the example to be followed.

And quite apart from these large helpings of standard procedure, the Queen and her royal relations are – perverse as the phrase may sound – very much the property of their subjects. Each adult member has a programme of duties which takes him or her incessantly round the country, and into direct contact with the public. This contact may be formal, with the obligatory handshake, the accompanying smile and expressions of interest in everything from boilermaking to microchips. Or it might be informal, with the sallying forth into crowds of curious onlookers, the eternal royal responses to a hundred questions, and the patting and humouring of children. More likely than not, it will be a combination of both.

When not within sight of the public, the work goes on behind closed doors; planning, speech-drafting, sundry paperwork, the eternal preparation and decision-making in response to the endless requests for patronage and the royal presence. And even when no official work – public or private – is involved, no member of the Royal Family can be guaranteed the same luxury of privacy which each of us takes for granted. As long as a ready market exists for any whiff of scandal or germ of gossip, upon which the disloyal ex-servant thrives as much as the unscrupulous journalist, no-one is spared the threat of intrusion. Even home can never be totally comfortable while the heavy police guards at every palace door, and the electronic surveillance on every wall, remind its occupants of the daily dangers of being royal.

The repetition of both duties and pleasures is to some extent inescapable for the Royal Family. King George V and Queen Mary were traditionalists at heart, and both lived by the immutable succession of ceremonies, State visits and public engagements interspersed by a round of holidays at Sandringham, Windsor and Balmoral, all in strict rotation: a "same time, same place" mentality which owed as much to the times as it did to their own respective upbringings and temperaments. Their lifelong obsession with birthdays and anniversaries was probably outrun only by the quaint custom by which all the clocks at Sandringham were kept half an hour fast, and by the King's intense Englishness. (His antipathy for foreign parts made it unlikely that his departures from the United Kingdom as its Sovereign ever got into double figures. "Abroad is horrible", he is said to have declared, "I know; I've been there".) His second son, and eventual successor, King George VI was very much of the same stamp intellectually but, with the help of a far-seeing and much more imaginative wife, came to appreciate the rapidly changing demands of kingship in an increasingly international society.

It was he who once described the Royal Family as a firm. Prince Philip has since referred to the family's periods of residence at Buckingham Palace as "living above the shop". Prince Charles has called the monarchy "one of the oldest professions in the world". If those phrases sound less dignified and too institutional for most people's taste, it is because the monarchy's members have come to terms with its role in a present-day society besotted with images and public scrutiny, and has responded, if somewhat reluctantly, with growing professionalism. There is today a controlled teamwork among the Queen's relations, and between them and their advisors and assistants. In all it makes the fusion of the traditional and the progressive palatable to them, as the demands of the twenty-first century draw near, as well as plausible to their people – both in the United Kingdom and the Commonwealth – and to the world beyond.

The Queen has led her growing team for over thirty years, and a competent performance it has been, too. Her accession at an uncomfortably early age may not have been unanticipated – her father had been a sick man for a full three years before his death – but the manner of it provided a weird, rather unreal beginning to her reign. No-one knows precisely when she became Queen, because King George VI died unexpectedly in his sleep one night, but what is certain is that she was, of all things, perched in a fig tree in Kenya, wearing bush slacks and a yellow shirt when the Crown became hers. By the time the news reached her, she was resting at a nearby hunting lodge, which had been given to her and her husband as a wedding present four years earlier and which has since been returned to the people of Kenya. For her first subsequent appearance – the initial leg of her hurried flight home – she wore no mourning clothes; these were stored in her transport ship then lying at anchor in Mombasa, and until they arrived even the Duke of Edinburgh had to borrow a black tie. When at length the royal party arrived at London Airport to be greeted by a sombre line of statesmen and watched by silent crowds beyond, the Queen, though dignified and composed, looked every inch the "poor lonely girl" who, according to her father's prediction, "will be lonely for ever".

It was a comparatively small family that she came back to. Its doyenne was the 84-year-old Queen Mary, who insisted that she, as "her old Grannie and subject must be the first to kiss her hand", and who herself would be dead barely a year later. Then came the grieving consort whose new title, the Queen Mother, would enhance the family image, and the one, unmarried sister, the 21-year-old Princess Margaret. Three aunts and an uncle – all in middle age – completed the tiny national "firm" then presiding over the country's national affairs.

For a 25-year-old to take over the supervision and effective direction of this family unit may have been daunting enough: for a woman by nature shy and by upbringing anxious to avoid doing the wrong thing it must have seemed positively oppressive. Yet today she stands at the head of a much enlarged family; its undisputed leader, its symbol and its oracle. Age and experience have transformed her. It is a sobering thought that the Queen has to date reigned more than twice as long as her own father, longer than thirty of Britain's forty-two monarchs since the Norman Conquest, and already half the span of Queen Victoria's unequalled period of rule. Whereas at her succession the Queen was the second youngest adult in the family, she is now the fourth senior in years. Then, she was the mother of but two young toddlers; now she boasts four grown-up children and is a grandmother three times over. Like Queen Victoria before her, she is seeing her dynasty secured in the direct male line to two generations, and by the time her reign reaches its end it may well be three.

Politically – or rather constitutionally – she has undoubtedly matured, an inevitable result of living through nine general elections, dealing with eight different Prime Ministers and coping with the invidious consequences of four changes of government. This latter she definitely does not enjoy. "It means knowing a lot of new people", she told Richard Crossman, the outgoing Social Services Secretary in 1970. "I suppose that's it", concluded Crossman in his diary, "All this simply means that, just when she's beginning to know us, she has to meet another terrible lot of politicians".

Meanwhile, that ever growing institution, the Commonwealth – a mere babe in arms of the vanishing Mother Empire in 1952 – has become a highly influential body of almost fifty members. Its successive controversies, such as apartheid in South Africa, Britain's membership of the Common Market, and the Rhodesian problem, have frequently strained not only its unity but also the Queen's delicate presidential position. Among those Commonwealth members are over a dozen countries who since their Independence have chosen to retain the Queen as Head of State, and again the recurring arguments for and against this state of affairs – especially in Australia and Jamaica, and to some extent in Canada and Papua New Guinea – have kept the Queen sensitive to the changing demands of the societies over which she rules.

That requirement in turn has meant an unprecedented amount of travel for her: indeed, she has left Britain more than sixty times to make over 150 official or State visits to a total of almost ninety countries throughout the Commonwealth and beyond. In fact, the changing style of the British Monarchy – which the Queen herself has encouraged – is nowhere better illustrated than in the comparison between her first grand tour of the Commonwealth, which was a six-month affair of leisurely ocean-going travel, to the present-day airline tours which enable her to enjoy her summer holiday at Balmoral to the full, visit Australia and half a dozen remote South Pacific island countries subsequently, and be back in London in time for the State Opening of Parliament.

The transition over the last three decades has left the Queen a visibly more confident, and certainly more authoritative figure than she was. That again is inevitable in a person sufficiently intelligent and enlightened to make full use of all the contacts and experiences of a relentlessly active, high-powered and varied life. As one who meets thousands of people, travels all over the world and scrupulously inspects every Cabinet paper sent to her from Whitehall, she is one of the best informed and most widely experienced people in the country. Though she may not overtly enjoy the daily chore of "doing her boxes", or the unceasing round of audiences with diplomats and politicians, she derives not only a sense of duty from these unavoidable necessities, but also the wisdom with which to influence those who may depend on her for it. Former Prime Minister

Harold Macmillan said that "she loves her duty and means to be a Queen". Another statesman, Sir Harold Wilson, has testified to that by referring to his audiences with the Queen during his eight years as Prime Minister. He was impressed to find that the Queen did not treat these meetings as merely social, and he was on some occasions nonplussed when she had evidently read more State documents than he himself had had time to digest, and was able to put him right or bring him up to date with information he had been too busy to collate.

The Queen's fastidious approach to her official duties shows through less in public than in private. Her inspections of formal guards of honour provided by other nations during her State visits, for instance, are primarily ceremonial, but her interest in the smartness and precision of the uniforms worn and the equipment carried by men of her own armed forces during ceremonial occasions in this country lacks nothing in intensity. She will not actually stop her horse at the Trooping the Colour ceremony to rebuke a soldier for disorderly dress, but any irregularity either in turnout or manoeuvre and, as one officer of the Household Brigade put it recently, "the Colonel-in-Chief will want to know why". That trait is not an acquired one; it has its origins in the Queen's obsession for tidiness as a young girl, which became a family joke the longer it persisted. Certainly there was amusement at the way in which, during a Privy Council meeting involving a reshuffle of cabinet ministers and a reallocation of their seals of office, the Queen "was rather careful, examining the boxes in a friendly way to see that we all had the right seals". And more recently she noticed that the clergy of several provincial cathedrals were wearing scarlet cassocks, the traditional prerogative only of royal chaplains and the clergy of Canterbury Cathedral and Westminster Abbey. The Queen not only insisted that the provincial scarlet should be changed, but also contributed £3,000 towards the cost of having it done forthwith. The *Daily Express* complimented the Queen on her victory: "Tough on the would-be scarlet clergy", its leader-writer declaimed, "who chance upon the Queen in her most royal mood".

For all that, the Queen remains a shy, even diffident character with many of those whom she meets in the course of duty, but whom she does not know. Like some of her recent forebears, both her own disposition and her upbringing, overshadowed as it was by the awful and inexorable certainty of ultimate responsibility, made her something of a loner – a fact which easily explains the absence of any regular male companions or escorts before her engagement in July 1947. Her loneliness kept her drawn tightly into her own family, a sure recipe for social restriction. Coupled with the fact that, unlike Prince Charles for example, she never had the opportunity to meet, far less mix with, people from vastly different backgrounds, this led the Queen to be unduly reticent with those she meets for the first time. Some people find it disheartening to watch her being introduced to long lines of people – be they statesmen or film stars – performing the physical duty of shaking hands, fixing a smile and giving a piercing though kindly look with those bright blue eyes, yet saying not so much as a "Good evening". The Germans were particularly disappointed when, paying her first State visit there since the end of the war twenty years earlier, the Queen seemed unsmiling in the face of the rapturous reception she received in the streets of Bonn. "Smile a little more, Your Majesty, please", pleaded one newspaper respectfully. Eventually, though one suspected reluctantly, she did.

Stories like these are all the more confounding when the Queen's great sense of humour is taken into account. Many people expecting the most formal of audiences with her discover not only that she possesses a sense of fun, but also that she uses it on the most unexpected occasions. It took the television personality Michael Aspel by surprise when he once asked her what she thought of the reptile house at Regent's Park Zoo. "An ideal place for an assignation, I should think", she replied. At the Prince of Wales' wedding in 1981 she could hardly contain her laughter when the choirmaster conducted one of the anthems so vigorously that he sent a choir-stall lampshade flying. At the following year's Braemar Games, the Queen insisted on shaking hands with Geoff Capes, the caber-tossing champion, who had warned her that he still had sticky resin on his hands. After the handshake she made a public show of pretending that her own gloved hands were glued together. And Dick Crossman recounted how surprised he was, after one Privy Council meeting, to hear the Queen describing an all-in wrestling match she had just seen on television. "The Queen was in tremendous form. It was interesting to hear what a vivid description she gave of the whole scene, writhing herself, twisting and turning, completely relaxed. It was quite an eye-opener to see how she enjoyed it."

It is not such an eye-opener, however, to see the Queen enjoying herself during her hours of public leisure. These days the ever-improving technology of television and still photography catches her spontaneity well enough and often enough to convince the common herd that her humour and, above all, deep interest in what she is watching – both qualities very highly spoken of by those who have met her – really do exist. They are most readily found whenever there are horses, and never are the Queen's gesticulations and facial contortions more eagerly anticipated by the cameraman than when she is watching Prince Philip compete in the carriage driving championships at the Royal Windsor Horse Show, or witnessing the finish of the Derby at Epsom. It is on occasions like these, moreover, that the Queen openly demonstrates that she is happiest and most relaxed when surrounded by horses.

Her enthusiasm for the Derby may seem surprising, and somewhat misplaced seeing that, in over thirty years of owning and breeding horses, the ultimate prize has eluded her – and never more tantalisingly so than in the first two years of her reign when Gay Time and then Aureole came second. In her unflagging efforts to seize the trophy, she supervises the breeding programme at the Royal Stud at Wolferton, and her racing manager, Lord Porchester, embarks on no change of policy without his royal employer's express consent. Time was when the Queen attended auctions and selected purchases. That is a rarity today, but she deals effectively enough from the office. In 1982, she sold one of her best fillies, Height of Fashion, to an Arab owner for over £1 million then used the proceeds – or part of them – to buy Sir Michael Sobell's training stables in Berkshire. The ideas were hers, and she saw them materialise into what Lord Porchester later called "a sound investment in bricks and mortar".

Nevertheless, recent years on the turf have been lean ones. The Queen still pays the occasional private visit to racecourses to see her horses run, but the days when to see her leading in winners was a regular treat have failed to return. In 1974 she crossed the Channel to see her filly Highclere run in the Prix de Diane at Chantilly. The horse won and, to the delight of the French who mobbed the Queen almost to the point of danger, she led her back to the winner's enclosure. Three years later she was overjoyed when another filly, Dunfermline, won both the Epsom Oaks and the St Leger at Doncaster, bringing the total winnings for the whole of her reign to around £500,000.

More recent disappointments have not lessened the Queen's love of horse racing nor her devotion to horses. Ponies were part of her childhood – her attachment to them probably even predates her own memory – and she saw to it that her children had every opportunity of riding horses, as well as learning how to look after them, from the earliest possible age. Princess Anne's son is being coached similarly, as, no doubt, will be her daughter Zara, and later still Prince William. Nor has the Queen's enthusiasm for riding been reduced by the fact that she is now in her late fifties. Any scavenging photographer can steal a picture of her riding through the woods at Sandringham in January, and recent photographs of her riding with the Princess of Wales suggest that the Queen has even taken up what seemed to be a hopeless challenge – that of encouraging the Princess to master horse riding again. Balmoral of course offers tremendous opportunities for galloping at speed in the wide-open spaces – the sort of thing the Queen used to do once a year down the course at Ascot – while the Home Park at Windsor is a favourite for the leisurely walk or trot. It was there that the Queen chose to invite President Reagan to join her for a much publicised ride one morning after breakfast during his stay at Windsor Castle in June 1982. However august the company, however, there is one odd royal quirk of nature which continues to baffle many of those who see tens of thousands of pounds spent on the Queen's personal protection. You will never see her wearing a riding hat while riding. The days when her neat, youthful, equestrian turnout was topped by a sleek riding hat are well and truly past. A headscarf is as much as she will wear, no matter how pointedly officials of the Royal Society for the Prevention of Accidents rib her. When, quite recently, she asked the director-general of the British Safety Council what his job consisted of, he replied that it partly comprised "encouraging you to wear a safety hat when riding, Your Majesty". The Queen was not amused. "I think I'm rather too old for that", she said – and moved on.

The Queen must be one of the few women in the country who is expert at riding side-saddle, and she has long since learned how to control a horse with the reins gathered in one hand. Trooping the Colour offers the only opportunity of a public display of this ability: for almost two hours she sits side-saddle for the journey to Horse Guards Parade, the hour-long ceremony itself, and the journey back. If you doubt the extent of her expertise, remember how effectively she controlled her mount Burmese after the shooting incident in the Mall in 1981, when the commotion of six pistol shots and the shrieks of terrified onlookers caused the mare to break into a bolt. The Queen had her calmed within seconds, and continued with the procession and ceremony without the slightest loss of composure. No doubt there were extra rewards for Burmese on her return to Buckingham Palace: the Queen personally feeds her horse with freshly-peeled carrots proffered to her on a silver salver as she dismounts. Only then will she go into the Palace to appear on the balcony and watch the RAF fly-past!

There are no prizes for guessing that the Queen's alternative passion for animals falls upon the Welsh corgi dog, a breed which has found favour with her and her family for over fifty years. She herself chose one from a litter of puppies in 1933 – though it was her mother who urged her to select the only one with a tail: "We must have the one which has something to wag", she advised, "otherwise how are we going to know whether he is pleased or not". The Queen has certainly been pleased with her corgis, which have been part of her life ever since. "Not nearly as nice as corgis", is her emphatic answer to anyone who tries to press the claims of other breeds. No Royal journey to or from Sandringham or Balmoral is complete without a cluster of them jockeying for position under the Queen's feet, and she has never baulked at the indignity of being photographed trying unsuccessfully to persuade one or other of them on and off trains, or attempting to untangle a clutch of leads while at the same time descending a flight of aircraft steps. Every morning, weather permitting, she will take a short constitutional in the grounds of Buckingham Palace or Windsor with three or four corgis at heel; they have been deliberately included in numerous official photographs; they are her constant companions at her desk, and even their occasional intrusion into formal company is tolerated. Their names have always been surprisingly cosy and unprepossessing – Susan, Crackers, Whisky, Sugar and so on. Only the name of the original purchase gave any hint of Royal ownership, and then in a somewhat scrambled form – Dookie. And in the private garden behind Sandringham House, a clutch of little gravestones shows that they each have their place of royal memory in return for their years of companionship. Though different members of the Queen's family have grown to appreciate different breeds, the corgi has never lost favour – and apparently can do no wrong. Only recently one of the Queen Mother's corgis vented his travel nerves on an airport official, and bit him. The Queen Mother was on the scene immediately – and comforted the dog!

On a less domestic level the Queen has her own kennel complex at Sandringham, devoted these days to the breeding of Labradors. These receive less public attention than the corgis, primarily because they are a commercial rather than a leisure concern. Even so, Prince Charles was photographed with his golden Labrador, Harvey, for portraits to mark his thirtieth birthday; some of Prince Edward's official coming of age portraits showed him with his black Labrador bitch, Frances, and both Prince Charles and Princess Anne can be seen at hunts or horse trials accompanied by other Labradors which first saw the light of day at Sandringham. When President Giscard d'Estaing of France paid an official visit to Britain in 1977, the Queen proudly presented him with one of her best black Labradors as a memento.

The Queen's love of horses and dogs is only a part – though admittedly the most readily recognised part – of her private life. She is a woman of comparatively simple tastes, despite the opulence which surrounds her, and her conservative nature makes her wary of undue novelty. The country pursuits which characterise her outdoor life – riding, walking, picnicking, accompanying the guns at Sandringham or Balmoral – are those customarily ascribed to the aristocracy, even if they do not exactly fall into the music-hall cliché of "huntin', shootin', and fishin'".

She has in the past been criticised, sometimes quite roundly, for doing nothing to discourage this 'horsey' or 'tweedy' image, with which many of her subjects, for want of the means or experience, have little natural empathy. But the Queen has always acted upon the principle that her leisure time must be spent essentially as she pleases, whether or not the media wish to seize upon and condemn it for the benefit of curious readers. She has made no substantial concession in that direction since the beginning of her reign: her patronage of race meetings and game fairs, horse trials and breeding shows is as strong as her unswerving loyalty to the headscarf.

It makes sense that way when you come to think about it. With every Easter and many weekends spent at Windsor, New Year at Sandringham, summer at Balmoral, the Queen is very much a country-based person during her holidays. And apart from the obvious historical and family attractions of each residence, it is primarily farming which keeps these establishments going. The Queen takes great interest in the commercial activities on all her estates and has sanctioned a number of important changes in the last twenty-five years in order to make them as efficient as possible. The enormous amount of vegetables and soft fruit required for banquets, official luncheons and dinners at Buckingham Palace are provided from the Windsor estate, as are many of the cut flowers and pot plants used to decorate its numerous grand rooms. Any surplus is sold to Brentford Market, as is most of the crop of mushrooms which depends on some twenty tons of horse manure from the Royal Mews. The Queen keeps two herds of cows at Windsor – over 200 Ayrshires and a pedigree Jersey herd whose offspring are exported as far afield as Oman, Brazil and New Zealand. Red deer transported from Balmoral, and a thousand sheep, graze on the royal farms there as well.

One of the Queen's priorities when she arrives at Sandringham is to inspect progress on the 10,000 acres of farmland cultivated under her supervision. Root crops, mustard seed, malting barley and wheat predominate, but there are also 800 cattle to produce beef on the estate, acres of orchards to produce enough apples to fill the baskets of some 60,000 pick-your-own fanatics every year, while Ribena, it seems, would hardly exist without the lorry loads of Sandringham's blackcurrants sold each summer. Meanwhile, over 40,000 acres of farmland at Balmoral produce barley and roots, together with grass silage and hay for the two herds of Luing and Galloway beef cattle reared there, while a small flock of Soay sheep, descendants of the flock rescued from St Kilda when the island was depopulated in 1931, provides the tenderest mutton for the royal table during the summer and those occasional long weekends which the Queen and her family spend there.

It is at Balmoral in summer that the Queen's immediate family is able to gather in profusion. The Queen herself likes to move there from London at the beginning of August, sometimes sailing around the south and west coasts of Britain in the Royal Yacht *Britannia*, to visit some of the Western Isles before calling in on the Queen Mother at the Castle of Mey in the northeast of Scotland. Otherwise, accompanied by Prince Andrew and Prince Edward, if they are in the country, she will take the overnight train from Euston to Aberdeen, thence to Ballater and Balmoral or, more simply, from Heathrow to Dyce Airport. Before long Prince Philip, who will have spent his customary few days at the Cowes Regatta, will have joined her, as will the Prince and Princess of Wales once they have completed their summer schedule of engagements in the south. Prince William goes with them, of course – thus providing the more vigilant members of the public with an all too rare sighting of him as he grows up. He eventually enjoys the company of his two Phillips cousins – particularly young Zara who is barely a year his senior – since Princess Anne and her children join the Queen within a week or so, usually before the Princess' birthday in the middle of August. Captain Mark Phillips has been a less regular visitor since the demands of his farmwork at Gatcombe have prevented him from moving north with his wife – a recent development that has caused periodic speculation about the state of their marriage. Princess Margaret usually spends her birthday – 21st August – at Balmoral, and the Queen Mother may eventually travel down from Mey to Birkhall, a small estate adjoining the main Balmoral territory.

The Prince and Princess of Wales tend to stay at Balmoral the longest. Prince Philip is more often than not off to Holland or Cumbria to compete in carriage driving competitions, then goes further afield in the interests of equestrianism or world wildlife. Princess Anne starts her round of engagements in late August, and Princess Margaret in early September. Nevertheless, and despite the fact that the Queen faces substantial amounts of work almost every morning, there is no lack of opportunity for the Royal Family to enjoy their time together. Tramping the estates to see work in progress is a natural diversion; the Queen, like Queen Victoria before her, enjoys rides into the hills; Prince Philip and Prince Charles, plus a few invitees, will take guns onto the grouse moors or, in September, stalk some of the 2,500 deer which roam wild there. The Queen, a practised and useful shot herself, may go with them as an extra gun, though more frequently she and the other ladies of the family will follow and supervise what are cosily called picnics, but which would amaze even the best established firm of outdoor caterers. The equivalent meal for a royal afternoon is a barbecue – a favourite pastime for all the family for over a decade, and one in which they all participate. They are now a regular part of the holiday routine, and allow the Duke of Edinburgh, whom Prince Charles has praised for his aptitude at outdoor cooking, full rein for his wide ranging and imaginative culinary skills.

On fine, clear days, a good brisk hike over the hills will take up the best part of the day for the Queen, while nearby Loch Muick has always been ideal for the royal children to paddle or go boating in. And the family as a whole is only a short car journey away from Braemar where the annual Highland gathering takes place early each September. Following a tradition set by Queen Victoria in 1848, the Queen and most of her immediate family, including Princess Margaret's children, attend as guests of honour and receive the annual tributes of heather from local schoolchildren. Something for everyone, it seems, at Balmoral. No wonder the Queen likes to stay there until the beginning of October if she can.

The call of duty is never far away, however. Among the dozens of private guests the Queen invites to Balmoral each summer is the Prime Minister, who normally stays for a long weekend. That visit is essentially a social one – a mark of the sovereign's esteem for the work of her first minister – but since it will have been a month or more since the last royal audience, the Queen will also spend a more formal session being brought up to date on the latest political and diplomatic developments. This, of course, comes on top of the work which intrudes upon every day's activities and which necessitates daily deliveries of paperwork from London by air, and the installation of a whole section of the Post Office at Balmoral.

Much of that work involves the last-minute preparations for the Queen's autumn engagements, which in recent years have usually included a major overseas tour. In truth there is nothing last-minute about the arrangements, which often take eighteen months or two years to perfect. Involving as they do long distances, a variety of different locations – since the idea of killing several birds with one stone has an obvious economic appeal – and, above all, delicate political considerations, the much publicised and important tours can never be too early or too fully considered.

Until comparatively recently, it was reckoned to be the rule that the sovereign never paid more than one official or State visit to any one country. But certain political developments – especially the growing importance of the Commonwealth and the British commitment to the EEC – have changed all that. Canada has received no fewer than thirteen visits from the Queen, Australia nine, New Zealand six. Fiji, Bermuda and Jamaica are among the other Commonwealth countries who have received her more than twice. She has visited France and West Germany three times, twice each as a State visitor.

Maintaining the unity of the Commonwealth has become something of a personal crusade for the Queen, and has led her to make certain of visiting every one of its members at least once, whether before or since Independence. By October 1982, towards the end of her South Pacific tour, she had achieved that aim – with the sole exception of Belize which had become independent the previous year, and which at present exists in such acutely vulnerable political circumstances that she is unlikely to be able to visit the country for some time.

Not that the Queen lacks the personal courage to pick up the occasional hot potato. In 1961, she insisted on visiting Ghana, four years after independence, in spite of intense political unrest there which culminated in an enormous explosion in the centre of Accra a week before she was due to arrive. The British Cabinet was in serious doubt about the wisdom of the visit, Parliament just avoided a division on the issue, and the press, no friend of President Nkrumah, bayed for the Queen to withdraw. "Impatient", as Prime Minister Harold Macmillan wrote, "of the attitude towards her to treat her as a woman, and a film star or a mascot", she went. She went, too, to Quebec in 1964 when the separatist movement was so strong that there were overt and express threats to kill her. They were tense days indeed, and a British public, already convinced of the possibility less than a year after President Kennedy's assassination, waited hourly for the inevitable. It failed to materialise, though the strain showed on the Queen's face as never before and rarely since, and her bravery was vindicated again. As late as 1979 she was fully prepared to carry out an arranged visit to Iran despite the imminent deposition, in potentially the bloodiest manner, of her prospective host the Shah. Ultimately it was he who backed out, pleading that he would not be able to entertain her fittingly. The Queen, of course, understood.

No royal visit abroad is lightly undertaken. Invitations from foreign hosts are carefully considered not only by the Queen and her advisors at Court, but also by the Foreign Secretary in whom may repose the last word on the diplomatic advisability of royal tours. Indeed, royal visits have been called off or postponed at a moment's notice: two of Princess Alexandra's visits in recent years, one to Mauritius and one to Peru, were postponed – the latter because the Falklands conflict intervened. In 1982 the Queen's State visit to Sweden was postponed because Queen Silvia was expecting a baby at about the same time. (The process sometimes happens in reverse: in 1983 the President of Sri Lanka's State visit to Britain was twice postponed – once because it coincided with the date of the British General Election in June, and again because the political situation in Sri Lanka later in the year made it inadvisable for the President to leave his country.)

Once, however, the invitation is accepted in principle, an outline programme is submitted to the Queen for her approval. Where possible, she likes to see a specific purpose by which the visit may be justified, though events sometimes fall short of intentions. One invitation to include Papua New Guinea in her South Pacific tour was based on the hope that the Queen would open the country's new parliament building, but long before she arrived it became obvious that it would be far from completed. On the other hand, the Queen may consider it only polite to drop in on a country for no better reason than that she is passing by anyway. Her 1982 visit to the Solomon Islands was not very different from her 1974 visit but she was going past the front door on her way from Papua to Nauru, and it seemed the civil thing to do. Her hosts like to satisfy the Queen's personal tastes as far as possible – hence the abundance of equestrian interludes in many of her tours – but she may make specific requests of her own. While in Australia recently she asked if a visit to the town of Bathurst, near Sydney, could be included in the itinerary because she hadn't seen it for thirty years and wanted to again.

When the outline schedule has been agreed, the Queen will normally send two or three members of her household – a private secretary, a press officer and a police officer – to the countries concerned on a reconnaissance mission. This comprises a thorough analysis of the places to be visited, the most important people to be met, and the route to be taken, as well as a consideration of timing, security and press facilities. In particular the Queen's accommodation must be discussed and agreed upon. Presidential or royal palaces and ambassadorial residences are most frequently used, though in an emergency the Queen has stayed at an hotel, as she did in California in 1983. But these days the Royal Yacht *Britannia* solves any accommodation problems on many major tours. Among its several advantages are a greater degree of security, the pleasant feeling of being in familiar surroundings even in the most exotic places, and above all the ability to accommodate a full royal party.

For it may come as a surprise to learn that the Queen and Prince Philip are accompanied on most large royal tours by three dozen or more staff. These include two Ladies-in-Waiting and their maids, three Private Secretaries and four clerks, two members of the Press Office, three equerries, two police officers, two of the Queen's dressers plus one hairdresser, five footmen, a page, a valet, an orderly and, last but doubtless not least, a travelling yeoman. And always, just a few paces behind the Queen, is her medical officer with a sizeable black box at the ready. Sometimes it seems he can't be close enough: tent banquets in the middle of the Arabian desert, open-air feasts in the steamy heat of Tonga, spit-roasted bats and blackbirds in Tuvalu and the obligatory swigs of kava, Fiji's ritually prepared liquid mud, must make the Queen's digestion a matter of periodic medical concern. Small wonder she carries Malvern water around with her!

National or cultural traditions are, of course, to be treated with delicacy. No-one realises this more than the Queen, yet somehow she has to reconcile the expectations of her hosts both with her own feelings and with those of people back home. In 1961 the Indian government arranged a tiger shoot for the Queen who clearly did not anticipate the uproar when a photograph of her standing beside her victim appeared in Britain. In 1974 she watched the tribesmen of Pentecost Island perform the manhood initiation ceremony of diving head first from the top of a high tower with only vines tied to their ankles to prevent them from hitting the ground. She looked sickened at the succession of spectacular near misses, and called a halt when one man crashed to the ground after his lifeline snapped. But she is game for most things. While she has never rubbed noses or smoked a peacepipe, she has stood her ground in the face of frighteningly earnest warrior challenges in New Zealand and the Solomons, patted lambs on the head in Nepal immediately before they had their throats ritually slit, and been borne aloft in a ceremonial canoe by twenty-six brawny natives in Tuvalu – though she confided to her local Women's Institute branch at Sandringham three months later that "It was a little queer".

Willing though she may be to participate in the unusual acts of hospitality, the Queen's sense of dignity, correct form and strict adherence to her programme rarely allows her to enjoy the unexpected, however well meant it might prove. During a visit to the City Hall at Brisbane, somebody had the last-minute brainwave of transporting a dozen koala bears from a local breeding compound and sitting them on the branches of five potted eucalyptus trees in the vestibule so that she could see them as she entered the building. That particular feature was not on the Queen's programme, and she dutifully ignored it as she made her way to the municipal reception arranged for her. It took a quiet word in her ear, and some crossed fingers, to ensure that she stopped on her way out to look at the koalas, and to have a word with their owners. During her State visit to Zambia in 1979, President Kaunda invited her, during her speech at a banquet, to clap in time to a song he chanted about ties between his country and Britain. The Queen looked distinctly uneasy and refused to play along. During the same visit the Mayor of Lusaka gave a speech which suddenly developed into a political tirade, then asked the Queen if she would like to reply. "No, thank you very much", she said.

That reply was instant and, like others given in similar circumstances, accompanied by the Queen's most effective social weapon. This is the impassive and chilling royal stare which contrasts severely with the broad and ready smile that lights up her face when she is genuinely pleased. Another of her favourite retorts to bad manners is the trick of taking the wind out of other people's sails. When, during her Silver Jubilee year, the recently dismissed Australian Prime Minister, Gough Whitlam, seemed to be taking malicious revenge by making fun of the Queen's titles and speaking of her as a potential Queen of Sheba, she refused to be drawn. "The Queen did not see anything untoward in Mr Whitlam's speech at all", was the official, damning reply. On the same tour she was relentlessly booed by those who objected to her representative, the Governor General, having the power to dismiss their Prime Minister – "A Queen is quaint, a Governor General ain't", said one placard. That was easy meat for the Queen. "If on occasions there has been a note of dissent", she said in her parting speech, "that is what freedom of expression is all about – a freedom sadly no longer enjoyed in many other countries"

She equally effectively squashed the formidable King Hassan of Morocco after he had rearranged part of her State visit at short notice in 1980, taking her motorcade along different and much longer routes than planned, keeping her waiting at State banquets, refusing to let her sit near Prince Philip, and insisting on her changing cars several times in the middle of journeys. Everybody expected the Queen to be glad to be leaving the country, but you wouldn't have thought it from the tone of her parting words: "We are very grateful for the close personal interest Your Majesty took in our schedule", she wrote. The laugh was clearly on the King. The Queen's tactful yet unmistakable put-down came a close second to the one she delivered to the students of Stirling University after they had jeered, jostled and insulted her during her visit in 1972. Replying to an official apology, she said pointedly, "The Queen has become quite used to behaviour of this sort". With one stroke she thus dismissed both the apology and the drunken bad manners which prompted it.

No set pattern exists either to the number or length of the Queen's visits abroad, though the tendency is to make them coincide with other people's spring and summer. That in turn often means leaving the United Kingdom in times of adverse weather, thus gaining both the British public's envy and full marks for a very sensible policy. It doesn't always work out like that of course, and sometimes the British weather follows her. Her 1983 tour of the West Coast of America, for instance, was a climatic disaster as rain fell almost every day and storms lashed the entire coast, causing problems for the Royal Yacht. But the Queen could afford to laugh at that: "I knew before we came", she announced mischievously at a State banquet given by President Reagan, "that we had exported many of our traditions to the United States. I had not realised that the weather was one of them".

The weather in any country to be visited is of course a factor in determining what clothes the Queen will wear. Temperature and humidity, and the frequency of indoor and outdoor engagements double and treble the number of outfits which the Queen must take with her, and thus the number of huge trunks and boxes, each labelled simply "The Queen", which are trundled aboard planes and ships in advance of the Queen's embarkation. But she is no fashion slave, and the old belief that she never wears anything twice is a complete myth. Sharp-eyed observers will have noticed that she does not necessarily distinguish her hosts by wearing a new outfit on every visit. One blue and green ensemble worn in Fiji in October 1982 was used again for her visit to the Cayman Islands the following February; a floral outfit she wore in Sri Lanka in autumn 1981 was seen again in Tuvalu a year later, and one particular cherry-red coat, dress and hat remained her favourite for almost three years. Evening dresses last even longer; a pale green gown encrusted with sequins and pearls, first seen in Silver Jubilee Year, was being worn more than five years later on a State occasion in Australia.

That, like many of the Queen's formal evening dresses, is embroidered by hand by dozens of employees of one or other of the Queen's dressmakers. The Queen orders her clothes from three main sources: the house of Norman Hartnell, which will soon celebrate fifty years of royal patronage; Hardy Amies, with a tally of more than thirty years royal service; and Ian Thomas, a former Hartnell man, who has been supplying the Queen for just over a decade. The Queen never visits their respective establishments to choose clothes or to have them fitted: they all send a huge selection of designs to Buckingham Palace and the Queen, in co-operation with her dresser, marks each with the single comment "Yes" or "No". From the approved items, combined with a schedule of the Queen's forthcoming engagements, the couturiers design up their suggested outfits, and present samples of material to go with each. Once the Queen has given her final consent to the combination of design and fabric, she can expect up to four fittings for each chosen garment, which means regular sessions of two or three hours, standing still or walking to and fro while each dress and coat is adjusted to perfection.

In the days when the Queen's day dresses were rather fuller than they are today, the periodic nightmare both for her and her designers was the sudden gust of wind which, whether at home or abroad, might cause an embarrassing ballooning out or, worse still, the upwards lift. Several possible solutions have been popularly suggested, many of them including the insertion of lead in the hems, or circulated as authentic. In fact, the Queen has long accepted that a full skirt cannot in extreme conditions possibly avoid flying up. The only feasible device is a straight underslip which, if the worst happens, will remain in place and at least minimise the embarrassment all round. The other perennial danger is the hat that is blown from the Queen's head in high winds. It actually happened in Oman. The Queen, standing in a fierce, gusting wind as the National Anthems were played at the beginning of her State visit there in 1979, felt the hat lifting, but was reluctant to detract from the solemnity of the occasion by striving to keep it on her head. Only when it actually left her head did she react, clawing it back with lightning speed. The hat was retrieved, and the gleaming heads of a couple of hat pins in each of the Queen's hats today shows that the lesson has been learnt.

Bad weather is certainly one of the less attractive features of Britain for any State visitor to this country. In general the Queen entertains two foreign Heads of State a year, one in March, the other in November. There are variations of course: London has seen the occasional State visitor in April or June; some, like the King of Sweden, have been entertained at Holyroodhouse or, like the President of Italy and Queen Margarethe of Denmark, at Windsor. Most land in Britain at Gatwick Airport, though some arrive at Greenwich or Westminster, having travelled by sea from the European coast. Once the visitor has set foot in Britain, however, the opportunities of variation are limited. Standard procedure requires that he or she visits St James's Palace to receive addresses of welcome from Parliament, Westminster Abbey to lay a wreath on the tomb of the Unknown Soldier, and Clarence House for tea with the Queen Mother. There will be lunch with the Mayor and Aldermen of the City of London at the Guildhall, a meeting with the Prime Minister, another meeting with a group of expatriates living or working in London. A State banquet given by the Queen at one of her palaces will be reciprocated by the visitor, usually at Claridge's Hotel. Only on the last complete day will the visit be distinguished by something of peculiar interest to the visitor – the Sultan of Oman went to see an army camp in Dorset, especially to witness British military hardware in action; Queen Beatrix of the Netherlands was scheduled to visit tulip fields at Spalding – though in the event the trip was cancelled.

The Queen's own programme of engagements at home is necessarily concentrated in London, where most of her constitutional work is done. For the purpose, she resides at Buckingham Palace usually from mid-February to the end of July, and from early October to Christmas. Her day will begin with an early morning cup of tea, brought to her bedroom in the northwest facing room on the first floor of the three-storey palace. With it comes a selection of the morning papers – including the *Sporting Life*, which she will probably turn to first. She possesses an encyclopaedic knowledge of both horse breeding and racing form, and has no intention of letting that slip. After breakfast, taken either in her personal suite or with the rest of the family, the Queen will take a quick turn in the Palace gardens – they comprise over forty acres – exercising the corgis as well as giving herself a breath of fresh air before the day's business begins.

The first visitor to her office – at round about ten o'clock – is normally her Private Secretary, who arrives with a sheaf of papers among which are details of the day's schedule, the more important documents concerning future engagements, draft speeches for approval, letters which the Queen will wish to read and take action on personally. They will discuss many of these matters on the spot, the Queen giving her instructions to the Private Secretary who will then liaise with other members of the Household as necessary. If any audiences have been planned, they will normally take place immediately afterwards, and indeed most of the Queen's mornings are consumed by the seemingly endless meetings with diplomats and other dignitaries. These may be British ambassadors or High Commissioners to other countries, or the ambassadors or High Commissioners representing foreign states in London. They may be on their way into their official posts, or on their way out. Foreign diplomats embarking on their stay in London will present their Letters of

Credence to the Queen, and return to Buckingham Palace to present their Letters of Recall when their term is over. All such cases involve a formal audience, in which the visitor will advance the correct number of steps towards the Queen, bowing after each series of paces. He will present any necessary documents to the Queen, who will lay them on a table beside her before engaging him in brief social conversation – usually on the theme of her own experiences of the country he represents. The Queen takes the initiative at all times, and herself decides when to terminate the audience. She does this by pressing a bell, at which the doors are opened and the visitor backs out as precisely and formally as he came in. The Queen rarely finds these audiences instructive or much fun: they are too brief and too routine to be of interest, and the mornings when five or six have to be processed must seem very long indeed.

A frequent alternative morning engagement is the Investiture. The Queen, as the fount of all honours, approves at least two Honours lists a year: one is officially announced at the turn of the year, the other on the Queen's official birthday. They are colossal schedules, usually filling two full pages of the quality papers with small print, and the drawing up of names is exceeded in terms of consumption of time only by the physical presentation of medals. The Queen undertakes this in two separate series of approximately half a dozen or eight investitures, one such series coping with each batch of honours. The investitures relating to the New Year Honours are held in February and March, those for the Birthday Honours in October and November. A presentation lasts approximately two hours, and on each occasion the Queen has to stand virtually rooted to the spot as over a hundred individuals take their turn to approach, bow and step forward for their presentation.

If the Queen is understandably less than absorbed by this intensely repetitive ceremony, she has yet to show it. She greets each approaching guest brightly, and pins a medal to a lapel as gleefully as if a lifelong wish to do so had at last been granted, then engages the recipient in a spot of congratulatory or enquiring conversation that seems both spontaneous and natural. How does she know what to talk about to each person? Easy when you know how. As the recipient makes his or her way towards the Queen, an equerry standing close to her right ear whispers brief details of the services which have prompted the award – whether it be to local government, St John's Ambulance or cricket. The Queen will normally have done enough preparation work for the reference to trigger off her phenomenal memory, thus enabling her to talk relevantly for the short time allotted before the next presentation. Rarely, however, does the assembled audience of recipients and their families hear what is being said, owing to a soothing musical accompaniment by a string orchestra in the gallery. Nevertheless, the Queen betrays a slight but noticeable tension: evidenced by the way she digs the fingernails of one hand into the cuticles of the other; it underlines her alertness and her anxiety not to offend or to be guilty of the merest mistake.

Thus may a single morning's duties come to an end, followed by an hour or so's break for lunch. Unless she has a public engagement which includes lunch, she will eat a fairly meagre and, above all, plain meal at this time of day. Again it will be in her private apartment, either alone or with Prince Philip if his schedule coincides. Alternatively, she may herself be acting as hostess, giving lunch to a dozen or so people representing a comprehensive cross section of society, and chosen for the honour of sitting at Britain's most illustrious table. Buckingham Palace luncheons are one of a number of innovations of the Queen's reign. Approximately once a month she and Prince Philip will sit down with public figures and celebrities, from chairmen of nationalised industries to actors and athletes, for an informal meal preceded by drinks and followed by coffee and conversation. They afford the Queen a relaxed and informal chance, all too rare these days, to get to know a little more about people in the public eye, and for them to appreciate something of her personality and hospitality. Sometimes they can reveal a surprising homeliness in the Queen. "I do wish he wouldn't do that", she once said when Prince Charles landed his helicopter close to the Palace, throwing up dust and small stones everywhere, "It makes the windows so dirty".

If the Queen remains at Buckingham Palace during the afternoon, further duties will almost inevitably be the cause. More audiences, more paperwork, fittings for clothes, sittings for portraits or official photographs, the occasional Council meeting, the signing of documents, successive conferences with Private Secretaries and Ladies-in-Waiting, or an appointment with her hairdresser in preparation for an evening engagement – all have to be fitted in.

Of course it is possible that neither mornings nor afternoons are taken up indoors: the Queen could easily be out in one part of London in the morning, and in another part in the afternoon. If her engagements take her to the Home Counties, she will as often as not spend the whole day in and around one town – Croydon, St Albans, Reading or Chelmsford for instance. When she is required to go further afield, she will often make her absence last for two days, staying overnight at the house of one of her few really close friends. Thus she may visit Manchester one day, then go on to Liverpool the next; or a day's engagements in Exeter will be followed by a further day in Plymouth. Scotland gets special treatment: every year at the beginning of July she spends a full week there, making the Palace of Holyroodhouse her base for six days of truly hectic business which allows virtually no time for rest – morning, afternoon or evening. The Queen has a special affection for Scotland, born partly of her family's long association with life north of the border, and partly of the tremendously loyal receptions the Scots invariably give her. "Our visit here is going very well, and Edinburgh is thrilled with all the pageantry" she wrote freely to Winston Churchill during her Coronation visit in June 1953. The visit was concluded by the singing of *Will ye no' come back again?* and she has indeed returned over thirty times since. It was in Scotland that she began her programme of Silver Jubilee visits in the United Kingdom.

For obvious reasons it was only in Silver Jubilee Year that the Queen agreed to visit Northern Ireland since the troubles resumed in 1969. Before that, her last visit was most memorably marked by a lump of concrete which was hurled down onto the bonnet of the car she was travelling in. In 1977 she was in something of a dilemma. Security considerations made it inadvisable for her to travel to Northern Ireland other than by helicopter, and the Queen did not – and does not – like helicopters.

With her characteristic respect for duty before personal preference, however, she opted to venture into one for the first time in public, and when she disembarked at Hillsborough Castle, she looked decidedly pale and uncomfortable. The remainder of her two-day visit was conducted behind and within stout walls, the Queen being spirited between one area of maximum security and another. She was able to show her face infrequently, and then only through the narrowest of windows. It is doubtful whether she slept comfortably during her overnight stay, but she had a few weeks earlier reminded Parliament that she "was crowned Queen of the United Kingdom, Great Britain and Northern Ireland", and she clearly knew where her duty lay as far as Ulster was concerned. It was by universal consent a brave and solid performance, which appealed as much to the British sense of adventure as to notions of royal dependability.

Silver Jubilee Year will long be remembered as a year of superb ceremonial, and it is perhaps in this sphere that the Queen feels most at home. As titular Head of State, she insists on opening each session of Parliament in person. It is the one ceremony of State that continues as a regular constitutional necessity throughout the reign, and being both a traditionalist and conscious of the historic and residual duties of the Crown, the Queen is reluctant to delegate this most symbolic of her prerogatives. Even when the snap General Election of February 1974 meant that a new Parliament had to be opened at short notice the Queen, who was then in the middle of a tour of Australia, was determined to preside at the ceremony. She returned in haste, performed the Opening, and resumed her Commonwealth visit in the first week of March. On that occasion there was not sufficient time to organise a full State Opening, but normally no detail of ceremonial is spared. Out come the Crown Jewels; the Irish State Coach, in which the Queen invariably travels for the occasion, makes its rare appearance; a second throne is reloaned by the Marquess of Cholmondely, so that Prince Philip can have a place next to the Queen – even if his throne has no canopy and it is an inch or so lower than hers.

This is also one occasion at which the Queen is as anxious to have as many of her family in attendance as possible, and as early as 1967 her two eldest children, Prince Charles and Princess Anne, were present for the first time, in addition to the Duke of Edinburgh. Then as now, they all sat alongside the Queen, their ornate seats placed carefully to acknowledge the precedence that one must give to the other. More recently the Princess of Wales has taken her place beside her husband, while Captain Mark Phillips stands to the side of Princess Anne. On the front row of the peers' benches are the royal Dukes of Gloucester and Kent; behind them their wives, plus Princess Margaret, Princess Alexandra and, very occasionally nowadays, Princess Alice. Of course, all these additional members of the Royal Family have their own busy schedules, and they can only attend when they have sufficient notice of the occasion. When, as a result of the 1983 Election, Parliament was dissolved and reopened with considerable speed, only the Duke of Edinburgh, Princess Margaret and the Duke and Duchess of Gloucester could be present in addition to the Queen herself. Other business kept the rest of the family away, including the Prince and Princess of Wales who were then in the middle of their tour of Canada.

The ceremony may be regarded as timeless, but the Queen is not averse to making changes. One of the earliest allowed press and television cameras inside the chamber of the House of Lords to record the Opening ceremony live; another reinstated the old ritual of Black Rod's journey from the Lords to the Commons to summon the Lower House to the Queen's presence. In the mid-1960s the Queen insisted that the dull and ponderous Civil Service phraseology of the speech drafted in her name should be leavened, so that today she reads a speech which, though she has not written it herself and may not even agree with its contents, is at least readable and understandable to the listener. Two more recent changes have shown examples of the Queen's personal concern for those participating in the ceremony. The late Lord Montgomery was relieved of the duty of standing for the entire ceremony carrying the Sword of State after he stumbled under its weight. And in 1982, she temporarily discontinued the tradition whereby the Lord Chancellor, after presenting the Queen's Speech to her, retreats from her presence by walking respectfully backwards down the steps to the Throne. Lord Hailsham's age and infirmity made it a tricky and potentially dangerous manoeuvre for him to perform, and the Queen suggested – indeed insisted upon – the safer alternative of walking forwards.

Trooping the Colour is, by virtue of its obvious appeal to the tourist, one of the best known annual public rituals, and is a particular favourite of the Queen personally. It is, after all, the Household Brigade's own birthday tribute to her, and she has repaid the compliment by never having missed a single ceremony. Neither the deaths of the Duke of Windsor and the late Duke of Gloucester, each within days of the 1972 and 1974 parades respectively, nor the torrential rain which fell throughout almost all of the 1982 ceremony, have prompted a cancellation. The Queen, who makes it her business to pay frequent visits each year to various units throughout the country of the armed forces of which she is the head, deems it desirable and significant that she should be seen receiving the homage of her troops on her official birthday, and leading them away to barracks at the end of the parade.

It is a family occasion too. Behind the Queen, as she progresses from Palace to parade ground, and during the ceremony itself, are the Colonels of the Scots, Welsh and Irish Guards who, by a happy coincidence, happen to be her husband Prince Philip, her son Prince Charles and her first cousin the Duke of Kent. Before 1980 her great-uncle by marriage, Earl Mountbatten, used to join the royal aides as well, magnificently arrayed in scarlet, his uniform heavy with medals and orders, and with a shining, low-peaked, gold helmet on his head. If you ever wonder how soldiers can actually see what is going on under those enveloping bearskins and casquettes, you are in good, royal company. On one occasion Lord Mountbatten, returning from the Trooping, congratulated the Queen on "a very good parade today". "How the hell do you know?" chipped in Prince Philip, "You couldn't see a damned thing under that helmet".

In addition to royalty on parade are the royal spectators. Above the arch which separates Horse Guards from Whitehall is a room once used by the Duke of Wellington, and where on occasions like this the Royal Family, children and all, gather to watch the proceedings. Foremost among them is the Queen Mother, whose own advance procession will have traversed the parade ground to the loud and appreciative cheers of eight thousand spectators, and whom the Queen stops to salute as she herself arrives for the start of the ceremony. It is only a personal acknowledgement, yet it is always looked for as a small but unmistakable public example of the bond between mother and daughter.

Then, on the balcony of Buckingham Palace afterwards, even the Queen becomes a royal spectator as the family gathers for the fly-past – the RAF's own way of paying tribute to the Queen on her official birthday. On this occasion all three sets of French windows are thrown open, for it is not just the Royal Family which emerges but also some of the Queen's more distant relations. These vary from year to year, but commonly include some of the Strathmore cousins from the Queen Mother's family; Cambridge relatives, such as the Duke of Beaufort and Lady May Abel Smith; the Fifes, the Carnegies and Ramsays, reminders of the lingering links with the children of Queen Victoria and King Edward VII; the ever growing Mountbatten clan; royalties from the former German principalities and duchies of Hesse, Baden and Hohenlohe-Langenburg, representing the families of Prince Philip's sisters. Additionally, the Queen will invite guests such as, on recent occasions, the daughters of the King of Thailand and the nephews of the King of the Belgians, to witness the spectacular view from the balcony.

Trooping the Colour marks the beginning of a week of royal activity which has remained almost invariable for decades. The Monday following is Garter Day, when the Queen, already removed to Windsor for the weekend, presides as Sovereign of the Order of the Garter over a private conclave of members in the Castle's Waterloo Room, before entertaining them to luncheon in her private apartments. The Garter is one of the few honours which are the Queen's personal gift, so the assembly of distinguished Knights is a particularly friendly and homely one. In the afternoon they all process in their magnificent, deep-blue robes and white-plumed hats, down to St George's Chapel for the annual service. Usually the Queen is accompanied by the Duke of Edinburgh, whose knighthood dates from 1947, while the Queen Mother, a Lady of the Order since 1936, is escorted by the Prince of Wales who was appointed in 1968. Significantly, if Prince Philip happens to be absent, the Queen will walk by herself, leaving her mother in the company of Prince Charles.

The Queen remains at Windsor for the rest of the week, since the Castle is less than five miles from the racecourse at Ascot, and Garter Day is followed immediately by the first day of the meeting known as Royal Ascot. Like Epsom on Derby Day, the Queen regards Royal Ascot as a festival not to be missed, and indeed if ever there was a horse racing event patronised comprehensively by the Royal Family, this is it. The meeting lasts for four days, and a royal carriage procession led by the Queen opens each afternoon's proceedings. The procession may consist of as little as three or as many as half a dozen carriages, each containing members of the Royal Family, their guests and the closest members of their staff. Royal Ascot has long been a byword for the more bizarre attraction of social eccentrics, both in headgear and behaviour, but the Queen and her family have never been party to the indignities of such exhibitionism. She and her female relations wear coats and dresses they would be content to be seen in on duty any day, and hats to suit everyone rather than to surprise or amuse a few. For they, above all others, can afford to go to Ascot for the racing rather than for the society. The Queen once said, "If it were not for the Archbishop of Canterbury, I should be off in my plane to Longchamps every Sunday". Four days of Royal Ascot on the trot is an eagerly awaited consolation for her studied obedience. What is more, they count as official engagements and are mentioned as such in the Court Circular. Nice work if you can get it.

Although the week between Trooping the Colour and the end of Royal Ascot is the social and ceremonial highlight of the year, there are others with which the Queen in particular has become firmly associated. As Head of the Commonwealth who takes her position seriously, she invariably attends the annual Commonwealth Day Observance service in Westminster Abbey in March, and as often as not her programme of visits abroad will be so arranged as to enable her to be present at the biennial meeting of the Commonwealth Heads of Government – Zambia in 1979, Australia in 1981, India in 1983. In late March or early April she will equally inevitably attend the annual

Maundy Service to distribute specially minted money to the same number of men and of women as the years of her age, so that since her Accession the number of recipients has more than doubled. Then in mid-April she will be at the Badminton Horse Trials – an event put on since 1949 by her former Master of the Horse, the Duke of Beaufort, a nephew by marriage of the late Queen Mary and a favourite kinsman of the Queen. The Trials provide a perfect excuse for another family occasion: the Queen Mother, Princess Anne and Prince and Princess Michael of Kent are among the *habitués*, with Captain Mark Phillips a regular and often highly successful competitor, and Prince Edward always keen to put his own horse unofficially through its paces.

May is the month frequently chosen for the ceremonial presentation of colours to one of the regiments of the Household Brigade. This may be done at Windsor Castle, Buckingham Palace, or more publicly on Horse Guards Parade or in Hyde Park. The Queen, as Colonel-in-Chief, takes great pride in making the presentation as a token of the important link between her and her personal bodyguard. In direct contrast to the might and splendour of such occasions, the third week in May sees the Queen again accompanied by several members of her family, inspecting the exhibits at the Royal Horticultural Society's annual flower show at Chelsea. The Queen of course can wander through the gardens of Buckingham Palace at any time, and admire the 250 or so different varieties of wild and naturalised plants and flowers which grow there, and she can clearly do similarly at Windsor or Balmoral. Despite this, and despite having admitted several years ago that she was "not particularly renowned for my green fingers", she spends an eagle-eyed hour or so wandering among other people's creations, shown at their very best before Chelsea opens to the general public.

The same month, or possibly early in June, the Queen will pay what is effectively her only public acknowledgement to the game of cricket, by visiting Lord's cricket ground during one of the Test or World Cup matches. Her arrival interrupts the game for twenty minutes or so as the teams line up at the edge of the field to meet her. On one occasion the Australian fast bowler Denis Lillee sprang a surprise as she shook hands with him, by producing pen and paper and asking her for her autograph. "Not in front of all these people", replied the Queen, who *never* gives autographs. Everyone thought that would be that, but a few weeks later Lillee, then back in Australia, received an envelope from Buckingham Palace containing a press photograph of the incident, duly signed at the bottom, "Elizabeth R.".

The Queen's patronage of other sports is hard to come by. She does not enjoy football, and prefers to send her relatives, in what appears to be a fairly strict rotation, to Wembley to present the FA Cup each May. Nor is she a devotee of tennis, and so misses most if not all of Wimbledon each June. Rugby, golf, athletics, swimming and indeed most other sports are not sufficiently to her taste for her to be seen watching them with any regularity, and only on the most auspicious day for any of them will her presence in an official capacity be deemed justified. The exception, polo, might understandably be put down to a natural extension of her interest in horses, and her enthusiasm for seeing Prince Charles enjoying himself at his favourite sport.

Being the month before the removal of the Court to Balmoral, July is a particularly busy time for the Queen and her family, and is full of recurring fixtures. There is the Queen's week-long visit to Edinburgh, and within a fortnight of her return to London she will invariably take the Salute at a performance of the Royal Tournament; that annual blend of technical know-how and military ceremony which runs for a fortnight at Earl's Court in London. The rest of the Royal Family follow suit, thus rarely is this highly popular show performed other than in the presence of royalty.

Then, from the middle to the end of July, the Queen gives a series of three or four garden parties in the grounds of Buckingham Palace. These are monumental occasions not only because of the prestigious venue and the numbers of royalty present, but also by virtue of the sheer scale and variety of the assembly. Anything from seven thousand to nine thousand invitees attend at a time, and guests from the humblest, lounge-suited local government officer to the most impressive-looking Commonwealth dignitary in the full splendour of national costume mingle in a kaleidoscope of moving colour. At first the guests form a series of snaking lines between which the Queen and other members of the Royal Family walk, stopping every so often at groups of people preselected for the honour of a brief conversation. Eventually they reach the royal tea tent, and the formation of guests gradually breaks up as people make for other marquees where canapés and the tiniest, crustless sandwiches are available as well as tea and fruit drinks. A useful tip for the would-be guest is that teacups are not refilled – only replaced if you should want more.

Barring the Braemar Games, the next two months can be relied upon for their conspicuous lack of events attended by the Queen in public, and October does not boast any quantity of royal standing engagements – unless, unusually, the State Opening of Parliament happens to fall in its final week. November sees two major occasions of remembrance: the Royal British Legion Festival, staged in the Albert Hall on the eve of Remembrance Day, and the Service of Remembrance round the Cenotaph in Whitehall the following morning. The Festival is a comparatively cheerful affair, its final act of worship following upon a colossal muster of dozens of units representing the armed forces and their auxiliary services, and a series of displays showing operations from armed combat to medical care. Almost the entire adult complement of the Royal Family attends the Festival, a black-garbed gathering in a royal box relieved only by the vivid cluster of poppies attached to jackets, uniforms and dresses. The Queen's presence at the head of the family is acknowledged by the singing of the National Anthem at the beginning and end of the Festival, and by the rousing three cheers given by over three thousand people in the hall as naval cadets raise and twirl their caps.

The following day's Service of Remembrance is one of unmitigated solemnity, in which the ceremonial is geared to the symbolism of the Queen's leading role. Members of the public contingents of the armed forces, diplomats, politicians, priests, choirs and bands, all assemble in fixed positions, gradually filling the roadway immediately around the Cenotaph, except for an area studded with brass markers. It is to these that, when all others are in place, the Queen walks out from the old Home Office for the wreath-laying ceremony. She takes her place, standing against the most forward marker, while members of her family – usually including Prince Philip, Prince Charles, the Duke of Kent and Prince Michael, but in 1982, for the first time, Prince Andrew as well – form a rank behind her. Those other royal relatives who attend witness the proceedings from balconies above, their number invariably including King Olaf of Norway, an exile in London during the last war.

A much happier annual occasion in November is the Royal Variety Performance, attended, under a roughly alternating arrangement, by the Queen one year and by the Queen Mother the next. Like most of royalty's visits to theatres of all kinds, this long-established occasion is staged for the benefit of charities, a fact which no doubt helps to make the rather overlong performance of three or more hours tolerable. Almost of equal length is the annual Diplomatic Reception given by the Queen and Prince Philip at Buckingham Palace each December. Again the occasion has no political significance, but rather symbolises in a very grand and sparkling manner the Queen's constitutional role as Head of State. Here she and many other members of her family will meet representatives of every diplomatic or consular mission in London, whether or not she has already received the respective heads of missions during her year of morning audiences.

Like July, December tends to be a month of intense "office activity" before the onset of the Christmas and New Year break. The Queen uses this month to complete her indoor work, and finds little time to appear in public. In 1981 for instance, there were only two days on which she undertook December engagements outside Buckingham Palace; in 1982, only four. But she always finds time in the middle of the month for what might justifiably be called the "office Christmas party", a private evening social held at the Palace, at which her entire household is present to enjoy food, drink and entertainment on a truly royal scale. It provides the only annual opportunity for, say a valet or coachman to dance with the Queen.

These days, the size of the parties is getting smaller. The tightening of the economic belt which has become a way of life in Britain for over fifteen years has not bypassed the Royal Family in their official capacity. In that time the Queen has ordered several efficiency studies into the use of manpower and resources at her official residences, and intense pressure in the financial supply in very recent years has led to the wholesale reappraisal of Palace administration. Within the last three years, for example, quite severe reductions in staff have been achieved by natural wastage, with existing personnel doubling up on their duties: footmen thus now act also as porters, kitchen staff are given additional and more general errands. In the overall drive towards greater economy, no sheet of office paper goes into the wastepaper basket unless both sides have been written on, all lights are switched off whenever rooms are even temporarily abandoned, and first-class post is much more sparingly used than before. A greater proportion of the maintenance, upkeep and catering work is now put out to commercial contractors, and additional machinery has been acquired to lessen the need to recruit staff. Even the royal stables are now bedded with old newspapers rather than with straw – it's cheaper and more suitable.

Though the brunt of these economies is borne by the people who serve her, the Queen has become accustomed to making her own, very real contribution towards the now persistent shortfall in royal allowances. The annual Civil List tends barely to keep pace with inflation, and then only because the Queen provides funds from her own private resources to the tune of £100,000 each year on average. Although of course the Queen's private fortune is enormous, and the majority of it remains untaxed and unaffected by the statutory impositions falling upon her subjects, her voluntary annual contribution poses the thought, "How long can the Queen afford us?" as an alternative to the well-worn question "How long can we afford the Queen?"

Not many years ago it was a standing joke that the Queen used to begin many of her speeches with the words "My husband and I". She even made her own joke about it when speaking at their Silver Wedding reception at the Guildhall in 1972. But it was, and has been the Queen's serious and constant intention to couple her own identity with her husband's, and to allow her reign to be characterised where necessary by his influence. History alone will reveal the extent and depth of that influence, but there can be no doubt that the Queen's early loneliness and inbred conservatism has been the perfect foil for the progressive ideas of her gregarious and questing consort. No history of the British monarchy in this century will be complete without a sizeable reference to the authoritative and imaginative contribution of the man who almost prides himself on having no constitutional position in the country.

He has a place of precedence, of course: the Queen saw to that at the beginning of her reign, in the first of a series of moves to accord him the recognition she has always felt was due to him. In 1957, just ten years after their marriage, and precisely a century after Queen Victoria gave the title of Prince Consort to her husband, Queen Elizabeth conferred the title and dignity of Prince of the United Kingdom upon the Duke of Edinburgh. Three years later, she had her family surname changed from Windsor to Mountbatten-Windsor – again a reflection of her indebtedness to him. The Queen now rarely says "My husband and I" as an automatic starter to any speech or broadcast. Perhaps there is no need. Everyone knows that, although they see less of each other than almost any other happily married couple, and although they keep that important step or two apart on public occasions, they are inseparable.

Despite being the husband of the sovereign, Prince Philip does not have a "job" as such. The lack of a set role is a blight to the conscientious members of the Royal Family – Prince Charles is always complaining about it – but to the Duke of Edinburgh it must have been doubly hard. Though he did not give up the job he had when he married the Queen in 1947 – he was then a lieutenant in the Royal Navy – he was ultimately obliged to when, shortly before George VI's death in 1952, he was called upon to help fill the many gaps in royal duties caused by the King's successive and lengthy illnesses. Nevertheless, even if he failed to find royal life quite as conducive to his naval ambitions as he would have liked, he lost no time in bending the old rules, forging a role for himself and justifying the widespread public approbation of his personal hard work, his support for the Queen and his inestimable contribution to the lives of many of her subjects.

Like Prince Albert before him, he has espoused only those causes which have genuinely interested him so deeply that he could legitimately take an active part in them without pulling rank or feeling an inadequate figurehead. "I have no intention of being a sitting tenant in this post", he told the National Playing Fields Association when he became President in 1949, a comment which could have been equally appropriate when, in later years, he accepted similar positions with other organisations – the Outward Bound Trust, Boys' Clubs, the Council for Physical Recreation, the National Maritime Trust, and so on. It may seem a pompous boast, seeing that he holds honorary posts in dozens of service units, is Patron of sixty organisations, President of as many again, and member in some capacity or other of some 700 more – between them encompassing almost every public and private activity, from cricket and model-making to the promotion of industrial education and the administration of libraries and museums. But that merely – if merely is ever a word appropriate to him – reflects without undue dazzle the huge spectrum of his interests and hobbies, which range from polo to aeronautics, and painting to industrial design. It may also seem an untenable boast, bearing in mind that there are only so many days in the year in which to justify the holding by one man of such a mass of high rankings. Then you look at the Court Circular, and find that he has squeezed up to half a dozen disparate engagements into one day, and far outstrips every other member of the Royal Family in his annual tally of public duties – up to four hundred in any one year.

Now, even in his early sixties, Prince Philip shows little sign of either slowing down or becoming set in his ways. The great, abiding passions that led him to found the Duke of Edinburgh Awards Scheme, and to undertake a four-month tour of almost twenty countries back in 1956, are still there. Today they manifest themselves mainly in his presidencies of World Wildlife Fund International and the International Equestrian Federation, which seem to take up more of his time than any other official activities, and certainly account for more of his foreign travel. In the former capacity he visits up to a dozen countries a year, more often than not piloting his own plane between one territory and the next, in order to inspect schemes to reintroduce wildlife into areas from which it has disappeared, to discuss the siting of dams or industrial complexes in regions where wildlife is threatened, or to encourage, cajole or harry national branches to raise funds for their own purposes. "This is a disappointment", he told the Japanese plainly, in November 1982, when he learnt that only £15,000 had been collected in a national appeal. In addition, Prince Philip makes trips to WWF headquarters in Switzerland for meetings and conferences, almost as frequently as you or I visit the Post Office.

In the same way, hardly any major international sporting event gets off the ground without Prince Philip's participation in the arrangements as President of the International Equestrian Federation. For many years now he has flown off to all parts of the globe, from Russia to South America, to attend meetings at which the details of sporting events involving horses – be it showjumping or carriage driving – are discussed as part of Olympic, Commonwealth or European competitions. He is an active participant as well as a model president, combining his sense of fairness as a chairman with the hard-hitting, crusading zeal of the genuine enthusiast.

His passion for good causes on a national and international scale has certainly enabled him to make himself useful – an achievement which may not be as easy to attain as it sounds for a person whose every action and thought is commented on critically. But it has made him less available as a companion to the Queen as time has gone on. Not so long ago, his continual absences from Britain spawned rumours of personal antipathy between the Queen and her husband. One suggestion ludicrously ascribed his 1956 World Tour to the consequences of a fit of sulking after a tiff with the Queen. A few years later the joke, "It is reported that Prince Philip is to pay a State Visit to Britain" did the rounds. His journeyings have all happened too frequently and too regularly for them to be misconstrued now, and the Duke finds he can go more or less where he likes when he likes without having the Press searching for ulterior motives.

After all, he works with the Queen on major matters concerning the organisation of the royal Household, and joins her for all the important royal occasions each year. He is a constant companion on every State Visit she undertakes – though it must be admitted that he skipped the end of the royal visit to Fiji in October 1982 in order to carry out some WWF engagements in Japan. For the State Visit to Sweden the following year, he didn't travel with the Queen from London, but met her off the Swedish coast on his way from Zimbabwe. It's all part of the constant dovetailing exercise that appeals to his sense of efficiency and, after all, contributes to a large saving of taxpayers' money. It is doubtful, for instance, whether he would have travelled to Ottawa in 1982 to join the Queen when, at short notice, she attended the ceremony to sign over Canada's constitution, unless he had also been due to visit America immediately afterwards. He is aware that those who make it their business to watch over the royal spending of public funds will swoop at an indiscreet move at the drop of a hat. The six-monthly Palace meetings to map out his programme of engagements frequently throw up the dilemma of travelling quickly and comparatively expensively by helicopter, thus fitting in four or five engagements, or plodding more cheaply by car and disappointing scores of prospective hosts each year.

Though he is used to seeing things done for him at the snap of a finger and thumb, Prince Philip is not one for standing on ceremony and is impatient of unduly conscientious protocol. While he recognises that it has a place, he will avoid it where circumstances allow. He will, for instance, not insist that Lords Lieutenant, whose job is to welcome royal guests into their respective counties, meet him formally during his routine visits to the provinces. When he is abroad, he has an almost morbid antipathy for people who fuss over him. During a visit to a nature reserve in India in 1982, he was informed that the arrangements regarding the number and order of cars were to be changed. Eyeing a large number of armed police, and suspecting a last-minute security decision, he showed intense displeasure. "All right", he said, wagging an admonishing finger at his hosts, "But no police. Do you understand? No police!"

At the same time he has a timely sense of the ridiculous – not least of the inconsistencies of his own position. He once mused on the advantage of being both Earl of Merioneth and Chancellor of the University of Wales. "If I were only Earl of Merioneth I would belong only to North Wales. As it is, the University has a foot in both North and South Wales, so I can tell stories about either, depending on how I feel." On another occasion, he presided at Lords Taverners' luncheon at Fishmongers' Hall to celebrate the raising of money for the National Playing Fields Association. As Prime Warden of the Fishmongers' Company, he rose to welcome the Taverners. As Patron of the Taverners, he then rose again to thank the Fishmongers for having himself there. Then, with one hand he presented the Taverners' cheque to himself as President of the National Playing Fields Association, accepting the cheque with the other hand and thanking himself for the Taverners' generosity. He even brought the Queen into one of his self-inflicted jokes when addressing the Welsh Guards once in Cardiff. "What is unique about this regiment?" he asked, "I will tell you. It is the only one in which the Colonel is legally married to the Colonel-in-Chief".

If it is easy for a royal speechmaker to be funny, it is even easier to be predictable and to make standard, bland statements. This is something that Prince Philip has never accepted as a policy. "Some people", he once wrote, "have a positive genius for saying absolutely nothing in the most charming language. I try to say something which is at least constructive". For the public, the keen personal interest he takes in every one of the engagements he chooses to undertake is underlined by the meaningful, informed and considered remarks – whether formal or informal – which he makes as the occasion demands. Whether thanking hosts for granting him the Freedom of a city or of a livery company, or launching a major broadside on shortfalls in education or industry, his speeches are invariably to the point, often pithy, and always heavily researched. It is this that his audiences appreciate, and which emphasises that, for royalty in general and Prince Philip in particular, the hours of duty do not begin and end with a car journey in the Mall. Behind the public appearance there is a great deal of hard work and organisation.

Prince Philip once said that to avoid giving offence can sometimes be "a ticklish business. I have come to the conclusion that when in doubt, it is better to play safe – people would rather be bored than offended". For all his efforts to be taken seriously, Prince Philip has long since come to accept, though not in a supine way, that outspokeness can and does lead to public criticism. It came with almost alarming regularity in the 1960s, when his famous "pull your finger out" speech to the captains of industry first nailed his debunking colours to the mast. For years afterwards, every one of his social or industrial statements was pared and dissected by the Press, high on a periodic fix of mischief, and desperate to engineer controversy. It became a national pastime which before long threatened to engulf the Duke: well-known figures like Malcolm Muggeridge openly labelled him "idiosyncratic" and "a buffoon". He has rarely reacted – though in 1962 he did call the *Daily Express* "a bloody awful newspaper" at a reception that was meant to be entirely private. In public, he sees no point in becoming angry and believes that "actions speak louder than words, anyway". He also doubts "whether anyone has ever been genuinely shocked by anything I have said; surprised perhaps, but it usually turns out that, within a year or two, the subject has become quite a normal topic".

Having said that, his only wish – perhaps like Queen Victoria's consort – is to be understood, and nowhere is he more misunderstood than in the sphere of conservation. It has been said *ad nauseam* that his support for conservation is inconsistent with his participation in blood sports such as deer-stalking and grouse-shooting at Balmoral, and the killing of pheasants, at Sandringham. His equally repetitive reply is that his concern is with the conservation of species, not the preservation of individual animals; and that his personal sporting proclivities do not endanger the respective species any more than eating meat threatens the cow.

Indeed it says a lot for a man of so many parts that, by and large, it is only in his pursuit of game that he has been the cause of embarrassment to the Royal Family. But it is, after all, a private pursuit and one which he will justify against all comers. And its potential for controversy by a national press which likes to manufacture its own perennial sensations is completely overshadowed by the Duke's assiduous support for his wife as the inheritor of the British Crown. For although he has taken a distinctive line of his own since shortly after her reign began, it has never knowingly been to the disadvantage of the Royal Family or the institution it serves. The occasional gaffe maybe – at one time he was always being criticised for making disparaging remarks about Britain when he was safely out of the country – but he has trodden the minefield of public opinion with confidence and precision. In doing so, he has completed the task of bringing the monarchy out of the nineteenth century, and is busy preparing it for the twenty-first. He is happy to leave the Queen to preserve the traditions and dignities which she more easily understands and with which she more readily sympathises.

Certain areas of activity have become his as if by right. He plays a large part in helping to run the Households, keeping a weather eye on budgeting and accounting. He almost personally runs the royal estates, and with an efficiency of which Prince Albert would have been proud. He has encouraged greater publicity for the Crown in an age which is becoming more dependant upon it. He is known to have been the moving force behind the successful film *Royal Family* in 1969, and he was the first member of the Royal Family not only to appear on a television programme, as he did when he gave an illustrated lecture on his World Tour in 1957, but also to be interviewed live. One more than suspects therefore that it was he who suggested that the Queen's annual Christmas broadcast should be televised, and that it was to him that she gave that fleeting, off-camera smile at the end of her first "performance" in 1957. It might be a disappointment to him that the Queen is only marginally more at ease in front of live cameras now than she was then. These days, her Christmas message is prerecorded: it allows greater scope, enables her to correct mistakes and, most important of all, guarantees her a smooth, stress-free Christmas Day. The Queen has never really relaxed when the cue is given to perform. In 1979 a live interview, following her tour of the Middle East, completely dried up when the interviewer lost his nerve and the Queen felt unable to rescue him. Prince Philip gallantly saved the situation, though the experiment was never tried again.

Prince Philip's intervention on that occasion was typical. He is always there to protect his wife from being either embarrassed or harassed. He gets visibly tetchy if too much is demanded of her, or if crowds become too pressing or unruly. She will serenely walk past a wall of abusive placards, while he will take up her cause by arguing or admonishing the protestors. She will give any mass of people the time of day, while he tears a strip off local police for allowing so many people to overwhelm her. And she will co-operate patiently with film crews, while he raps out the order, "Don't bring your bloody cameras so close to the Queen!"

If it is to the Duke of Edinburgh that the Queen owes much of the monarchy's present-day respect and popularity, it is to her eldest son Prince Charles that she has been imperceptibly turning to ensure that those benefits continue into the next reign and the next century. Typically, it was Prince Philip who prepared him for it, insisting that he should become the first heir to the Throne to go to school with other boys, and more significantly that he should enrol at Gordonstoun, where academic studies are not the be-all and end-all by any means. Prince Philip also prompted his son's entry into the Navy and his initiation with the RAF and Royal Marines, and he encouraged the use of television and radio to launch him at the time of his Investiture in 1969 as a personality to be projected to a curious, yet well-meaning and protective public.

The result is a confident, useful and caring heir-apparent, who has come to terms with his position, his future and the age in which he lives – even though he admits that "rapid change is something I find difficult to keep up with". In less than fifteen years, however, he has brought the monarchy not just notionally but perceptibly down to the level of the man, woman and child in the street. "I'm delighted to be called Charlie", he once said, "It's better than in America where they call you Prince. You do get fed up with being referred to like an RAF police dog".

Like his mother before him, he has not made any really firm personal friends – his position is just too delicate for that, and he is in any event the first to confess that he does not find making friends all that easy. But he has found his solace in a wider and much more rewarding friendship, tangible and invariably noisy, with the people he will one day rule. For over a decade he was the most popular member of the Royal Family after the Queen, his genial grin and ready conversation with all and sundry showing an enviable combination of aristocratic bearing and down-to-earth modesty. Wealthy and privileged, mature and intelligent, well-travelled and well-groomed, he succeeded in that time in earning the admiration of his own sex and more than justifying that succession of public stolen kisses by members of the opposite sex, from young girls to grannies.

Prince Charles has inherited his mother's reverence for the Crown and its traditions in equal measure with his father's understanding of people, events and issues and his thirst for knowledge. If anything, his interests tend to veer towards the traditional; there is in him no technocrat screaming to be released, no engineer yearning for the opportunity to design and refine. He is not at home with mechanics or microchips, though he has unstinting admiration for those who are, and he publicly supports inventiveness in those fields. He admires personal endurance – a clear legacy of his life at Gordonstoun and its Australian counterpart, Timbertop. In his time, he has pushed himself to the limits: weeks of sheer hell as a Marine Commando trainee, physical collapse while playing polo in tropical temperatures, the dangers of parachuting and steeplechasing. Even the well-oiled machinery of royal duties falls prey to his overenthusiasm. His right hand on occasions becomes swollen through an excess of handshaking – once, he had to use his left hand to greet people – and he has fallen asleep during public engagements as a result of pushing himself too hard, probably against the advice of his staff.

His devotion to his public duties is rapidly leading to a yearly schedule as intense and varied as that of his father. Prince Charles has already notched up a tally of honorary positions, including over a dozen regimental Colonelcies and scores of chairmanships. He is Patron of a hundred associations, President of a hundred more. He casts far and wide with his largesse, which he will bestow on no unworthy beneficiary, nor for a moment longer than necessary. He has seen the *Mary Rose* brought to the surface – now it is time for something else. He has supported the United World Colleges until its immediate goals have been achieved – now he has cried off in search of fresh causes. They have never been backward in coming forward, but the main theme running through his intentions has been to improve the lot of the alienated, the disadvantaged, the young, and combinations of all three. The Prince's Trust and Operation Drake have been his main vehicles for doing so, and tens of thousands of pounds have gone in penny numbers to help hundreds of groups of young people in their efforts to raise themselves above the social deprivation of inner cities and black ghettos.

His caring attitude is not put on for the sake of the public. It is a natural characteristic. Prince Charles is a sensitive, thoughtful person who is by upbringing and inclination devoted to his own family – "very special people" he once called them. Of his "wise and incredibly sensible parents" the Queen is "just a marvellous person and a wonderful mother", while Prince Philip "lets you get on with what you want to do – an influence of great wisdom". By nature drawn to older people, Prince Charles, it will come as no surprise, was inordinately fond of his great-uncle Earl Mountbatten, whom he called his "honorary grandfather", and was devastated when he was assassinated. No surprise either that he adores his grandmother, the Queen Mother – "one of those rare people whose touch can turn everything to gold". A vast disparity of temperament has not prevented him from being close to his sister Princess Anne, while his relationship with his two brothers, beautifully illustrated by the fact that he wrote a storybook *The Old Man of Lochnagar* for them when they were children, is now emerging from a rather paternalistic one to one of equal partners. Prince Andrew's ordeal in the Falklands, and now Prince Edward's year in New Zealand and more recent spell with the Royal Marines have proven to the elder brother that here are men after his own heart.

Since 1981, of course, his heart has been elsewhere and it is now almost out of date to talk about Prince Charles without mentioning the lady responsible for the current, surging interest in the Royal Family. Diana, Princess of Wales is without doubt the most exciting thing that has happened to the British monarchy in decades. She came onto its very public stage at a time when few of its leading personalities could claim the advantage of youth, and she did so with complete confidence. She had "no doubts at all" about what she was taking on in marrying Prince Charles, and although that seemed a naive sentiment for a 19-year-old girl to voice, she has, in almost everything she has undertaken in the name of that great institution, shown complete self-control and assertiveness.

There is of course nothing the British public likes better than the vulnerable, waif-like do-gooder who looks in need of protection, and for over a year after her engagement, Diana was treated fulsomely and rather patronisingly as a public *protégée*. They were asking too much of her, getting too close to her, talking and writing too freely about her, and it was time it stopped – this was a general public attitude. The so-called taped telephone calls between Prince Charles and his fiancée while the Prince was in Australia, and the dozens of photographers who swarmed around her during the last days before her engagement were cited as examples of situations with which she could not cope. Apart, however, from dissolving into tears once, she showed that she was nobody's soft touch, nor incapable of looking after herself. She had already shown tremendous self-possession during the hectic days before her engagement, when she was almost daily harried by photographers and reporters in London, and only slipped up once when she unwittingly allowed herself to be manoeuvred into a position where a photograph taken of her against the light showed rather too much of her figure for her liking. She had responded with just the right blend of modesty and feminine charm to the sudden request by a schoolboy to be allowed to kiss her hand. And at her wedding, she looked after not only herself, but also her father who was determined despite illness to take her up the aisle. She gripped him firmly by the arm to keep him straight, upright and on course for that long walk together. "She was a tower of strength", he said afterwards. She may have got the order of Prince Charles' names wrong later in her responses to the Archbishop's questions, but even with 700 million people watching, it didn't seem to matter: it even seemed to heighten her so-called vulnerability.

"What I need", the Prince had said in 1979, "is a good wife". If his subsequent pronouncements are to be believed, he is more than satisfied with his choice. "My dear wife", he called her on the day she announced her pregnancy, "who has such a wonderful effect upon everyone". "I was indeed lucky enough to marry her", he said sixteen months later and 12,000 miles away. He loves to tease her in public because he knows she is easily embarrassed: "I wish we could have gone to a place near here called Great Tickles West", he announced to dinner guests one evening in Canada, and eyed Diana with mock lechery. She blushed, as she always does, deeply and uncontrollably. Sometimes, seated safely behind him, she will roll her eyes heavenward as if seeking some inner strength, or pull some kind of vengeful face at him. On one occasion in Tasmania, he saw it. "It's surprising what ladies do when your back is turned", he said.

At the same time, the Prince has never hidden his concern that his wife should make a complete success of her new role. Since their marriage – indeed even a little beforehand – he has been anxious for her to get to know the ropes of the royal job quickly and thoroughly, and although she was schooled primarily by the Queen's senior Lady-in-Waiting, Lady Susan Hussey, Prince Charles has always felt it his duty to be her guide in the field, as it were. The occasional nod or wink will confirm a correct move; a slight frown indicates a wrong one. It has many times been noticed how he keeps an eye just a few feet forward or a few seconds ahead of what is actually going on, so that he can prompt his wife where necessary. If he thinks she is coming under too much pressure, particularly if time is short, he will leave the crowd he is talking to, have a word with his detectives, then go over to consult with Diana to decide upon the next move. In this way, she is easily and tactfully rescued from overenthusiastic crowds which tend to slow her progress. The Prince's concern and his admiration show no sign of flagging. The devoted husband taking up his young wife's hand and kissing it is almost a regular sight, as is the hand slipped furtively or unconsciously round the waist as they make for their car or board a plane. And every photographer's prize is the chance meeting of eyes between man and wife in a fleeting private moment amid a whirl of a whistle-stop, meet-the-people visit.

Diana learned quickly and comprehensively about the life she married into. Hardly ever has she put a foot wrong, done or said anything remotely inappropriate, or embarrassed her hosts or her guests. There are rumours of course, the most sinister of them bent on creating or accentuating differences between her and her husband. She has nothing like the "overdeveloped sense of history" to which Prince Charles readily confesses. She does not share his passion for classical music, though she will dutifully go with him to hear it played or sung. On the other hand, he is no great fan of pop, but has been to more pop concerts since he married than ever he did beforehand. Although Diana will willingly watch him play polo and, like him, is a good skier, she is a fretful horserider and is said to have put a stop to his steeplechasing. Nor is she particularly at ease on the grouse moors or where the deer roam. All in all, there is an intellectual gap, generally acknowledged to be quite wide, and it has given many reporters the cue for creating endless tales of arguments at Sandringham and sullenness at Balmoral. According to them, she soon gets bored with her Balmoral holiday, with its domestic formalities and the kilted solemnity of the company, the interminable days of hunting, shooting and fishing and, worst of all, the weather – cool at best, unceasingly wet at worst. It got to the point where one columnist claimed to have it on good authority that Diana was "a monster and a fiend", making Prince Charles desperately unhappy in a marriage he could not now escape from.

There were even stories that Diana had been at loggerheads with the Queen, refusing to accept some of her gifts, including a gun dog, because of its association with blood sports; later insisting that her baby should be born in hospital rather than in Buckingham Palace; later still battling to be allowed to take Prince William with her to Australia. Like most insights into life inside the Palace walls, the stories have all turned out to be false. The Queen, who after all has known Diana from a baby, totally approved of Prince Charles' choice, and has been fairly bowled over by her daughter-in-law's success. Once the Privy Council had given its formal consent to the marriage, the Queen was photographed with Prince Charles and his fiancée, and the photograph was issued immediately for publication. At the Queen's invitation Diana attended several royal occasions before her marriage, including the State banquet given by the King of Saudi-Arabia during his visit to Britain in June 1981, and the Queen decided to include Diana prominently in that year's

Christmas message, making mention of the wedding and showing film of her new daughter-in-law taking part in a ceremony to hand over specially designed cars to disabled people.

Both the Queen and Diana herself were naturally aware from the very start of the danger that Diana's instant popularity might upstage the Queen, and to a certain extent this has proved the case. It is a fair bet that at least 75% of all the words and pictures published about the Royal Family since February 1981 have concentrated on Diana, and that, given the choice on the rare occasion when the two ladies appear together in public, the spectators will crane their necks more strenuously to see the new recruit rather than the established figurehead. One guest at a royal garden party in the summer of 1981 noticed how the polite applause when the Queen emerged from the Palace turned to rapturous cheering as Diana appeared subsequently. The Queen looked decidedly unamused, though she knew then, as she has always known that, with the Royal Family in the personalities business whether they like it or not, the novelty of an addition to the family can always take some time to wear off.

In fact the Queen has been a particularly solicitous mother-in-law, anxious to preserve Diana's legitimate privacy, and thus her personal happiness, during the initial period of intense and unrelenting interest in Britian's new princess. She has issued several public statements deploring Press intrusion upon Diana's holidays abroad and weekends at home, and even went so far as to summon the editors of Fleet Street newspapers to Buckingham Palace to request in the strongest possible terms that the harassment should cease. In doing so, the Queen risked the personal confrontation which in fact materialised. One editor is said to have told her to her face that he had no intention of complying with her request, and that Diana should perhaps send a footman out to the shops next time she wanted to buy wine gums.

It certainly did not stop some newspapers from sending photographers to Eleuthera, and again to Liechtenstein, to cover successive private holidays, while the grounds of Sandringham and Balmoral are these days thick with the men of the Press who spend weeks at a time skirting the estates in the hope of the picture that will sell round the world. Their activities being for the most part perfectly legal, there is no point in any member of the Royal Family having a stand-up row with them over the fence, but Prince Charles' anger does get the better of him when an excess of photographic zeal on a public occasion gives him the excuse to berate the Press on behalf of himself and, much more frequently, his wife. He has not yet made use of his sister's blunt and uncompromising expressions, but one sometimes feels the time cannot be far off when he does.

Diana of course feels bound to maintain a discreet silence, indicating her disapproval only by a thunderous look, an unco-operative attitude or a turned back. However she is not above giving any member of the Press a piece of her mind when the opportunity arises, and on one occasion at the beginning of her tour of Canada she lamented freely on her "trials and tribulations at the hands of the wolf-pack-like British tabloid press. When they write something horrible, I get a horrible feeling right here", she added, prodding her chest, "and I don't want to go outside". She reckoned that it would take her five or ten years to get used to it – a neat way of saying she knows what's in store and intends to stick it out and win. So much for the vulnerable Princess. Another cliché, the fashionable Princess, has lasted longer and with more justification.

Before her engagement she was, naturally enough, an unremarkable dresser. If her style of dressing could be put into any particular category, it was that of the now celebrated Sloane Ranger, but even she would disclaim the somewhat artificial sophistication of that easily applied label. Pleasant but unspectacular dresses; feminine, quietly shaded blouses; jackets and woollens in sober colours – these were the clothes in which she first came to the attention of the British public. Jeans and something a bit jazzier for weekend wear, perhaps, but never was the impression given that she spent long hours in front of mirrors or flitting eternally from shop to shop in search of just the right thing.

Now things are different. Within two years she blossomed into bursts of new colour and sometimes delightfully extravagant lines, creating a distinctive personal style and a way of wearing it which has almost given her name to an era in fashion, and wrested the royal fashion initiative, just when there seemed no-one around to take it, from the likes of the Duchess of Kent and Princess Michael.

More important, she is generally reckoned to have given a tremendous shot in the arm to British fashion houses. Unlike the Queen, Diana does not restrict her custom to a select few. Her designers of dresses alone number over twenty; hats, shoes and accessories account for another score. Many of then are off-the-peg purchases and nearly all of them British. If she can, though it's becoming more and more difficult as the word gets round, she will do much of her own shopping, visiting four or five establishments in Knightsbridge or Chelsea on each of several mornings or afternoons, in preparation for a new season or a royal tour. These shopping sessions are often referred to in the Press as "sprees", as if the urge has suddenly got the better of her and recklessness is the order of the day. In fact, as with any member of the Royal Family, a huge amount of preparatory work goes into the making of short lists of ideas to correspond with the use to which the clothes will eventually be put. In September 1982, for instance, everyone thought Diana had gone over the top when she appeared to have stormed out of Balmoral and was supposed to have spent £50,000 in one of these clothes-buying sprees. The story has been discredited now, and though there were substantial purchases, they were all for the forthcoming autumn season and the following year's tours of Australasia and Canada. Every dress, skirt, blouse, hat and pair of shoes had been carefully considered, and when each came to be worn, not one was seen to be ill-chosen or out of place.

As a result, she can look as regal as the rest of them when the occasion demands, in sumptuous silk evening gowns glittering with colour and topped with one of the two tiaras she now possesses – one a Spencer family heirloom, the other given to her by the Queen as a wedding present. At the other end of the scale, she can almost throw on a skirt and blouse for an informal afternoon at Wimbledon or a polo match, and go back to looking like the girl next door again. In a sense it is an extension of the royal tradition: the Queen in her day was able to swap a tiara for a headscarf, the Queen Mother her slingbacks for waders, Princess Anne her smart, pleated miniskirts for jodhpurs. The Princess of Wales has been doing her equivalent for almost three years already, and neither she nor her public have grown tired of it.

Nor has anyone grown remotely tired of her inventive way of carrying out her duties. If the Queen is to be acclaimed for instituting the royal walkabout, then Diana must take the credit for having inaugurated the talkabout – a system voluntarily and imperceptibly evolved, by which a little everyday gossip and the occasional wisecrack adds spice to the mere presence of royalty among its subjects. Diana has made the practice so popular that it now often becomes the focal point of any public engagement. The mysteries of bottling plants and sweet making factories may be fascinating for those most closely concerned, but the highlight of her visits to such places is the now inevitable stroll she takes along lines of spectators before and/or after her inspections. It offers to anyone who has had the patience to wait for hours in a prime position, perhaps the only opportunity of a lifetime to shake hands with her, to present her with a flower or a gift, to speak to her or merely to see her at close quarters. The effect on some people can be unbelievably irrational – the involuntary squeal of triumph at having exchanged a word, the mental blackout immediately afterwards, the hand that has grasped the royal palm held high, as its owner declares that it will not now be washed for a month.

In two respects, Diana does not follow the typical royal form when meeting the public. It has long been acknowledged that, if you are in a crowd and want to be noticed by royalty, you wear or wave something particularly colourful or outstanding – it gives the visitor something to latch onto by way of conversation. Princess Diana needs no such assistance. With hand outstretched, she dives straight into crowds, passing the time of day with unashamed blandishments – "Have you been waiting long?" or "What a lot of you there are", or "I hope you've managed not to get too wet". Somehow, they all develop into a chat and usually a laugh. The other variation on a royal theme is that with Diana, the rule that you never speak to royalty unless they speak to you first doesn't count, at least as far as these informal walkabouts are concerned. It never really stood a chance since she first came within earshot of a crowd. "Over here, Lady Di", they shouted then and still shout now, disregarding her new title. When she complies, they bombard her with greetings or questions before she's had a chance to say anything.

To some degree, the trend was already in sight during Prince Charles' last years as a bachelor, and the Queen and Prince Philip presumably grew accustomed to the sight of him becoming public property so tangibly. But the receptions accorded his wife must have worried them. Only recently has Diana's personality cult shown any sign of subsiding, and then only marginally, but for most of her few years in the public eye she became something of a latter-day goddess, swarmed over by the world's journalists and adored by an insatiable public. Some observers have likened her receptions to Beatlemania, but the raising of its members to the level of a pop star is not the sort of reaction the Palace wants to encourage. Fortunately, Diana has been able to take it all with a pinch of salt, never letting any of it go to her head. She has refused to play up to excessive adulation and has always moved on before things got out of hand. Accordingly she has rarely got herself into an embarrassing situation, and for someone not born into the job that is a remarkable record.

Of course, she became even more of a heroine when, in 1981, it was first announced that she was pregnant. As she and her husband drove through London on that crisp November day, Prince Charles was the butt of good-natured comments from a crowd congratulating him on his speed, manliness and general good fortune, but the Princess became the object of everyone's admiration. Twenty years old, attractive, competent, the wife of one future king and the mother-to-be of another – it all seemed too good to be true. And, unlike all other royal pregnancies, this one became, like Diana herself, a national chattel. For seven and a half long months, everyone talked about it, every newspaper and magazine offered information and advice. Gifts poured into Buckingham Palace, and could be coped with only after a special department had been set up. The Palace Press Office was kept busy with endless enquiries.

Meanwhile, in another fit of innovation, Diana decided that royal pregnancy purdah was not for her, and the old myth that royal ladies had to be kept out of action and under wraps for months before their confinements was blown forever. She was on public duty until a month before Prince William's birth, facing the tail end of a six-month barrage of questions and tips from children and housewives – the latter delighted at the way she shared the thrill of prospective motherhood with them. Even after that, she was a frequent visitor at Smith's Lawn to watch Prince Charles play polo, her no-nonsense attitude towards her ballooning maternity dresses contrasting starkly with royal attitudes of less than two decades before. By her decision, which many thought inappropriate at the time, Prince William should become the first British monarch to have been born in hospital, and her celebrated public appearance with her baby in her arms outside the hospital less than twenty-four hours after his birth was another departure from tradition long regarded as sacrosanct. How things are changing.

Diana has naturally been inundated with requests to become Patron of charities and other associations country-wide. Partly because of her early pregnancy, partly because two time-consuming royal tours took her out of the country, and partly because she is still being advised not to take on too much too early, she has accepted fewer than a dozen such invitations. Over half of them reflect her interest in children, and the well-known playgroup connection of her bachelor days. Similarly, the majority of her engagements tend to gravitate towards the *milieux* in which children are important – maternity units, special schools, adventure playgrounds, children's hospitals and so on. Now that her first pregnancy is over, and the long-standing vow to visit Australia, New Zealand and Canada has been honoured, the Princess will find her engagement diary progressively fuller during the months of general royal activity. As she is able to make herself more available, so the spectrum of her engagements will widen. Soon, for instance, she is almost certain to take up honorary positions in national and Commonwealth organisations, major charities, the armed forces, universities and polytechnics. She has already set up a Princess of

Wales' Charities Trust Fund, ready to receive some of the proceeds of gala occasions which she attends, for distribution to worthy causes. Gradually, as her consciousness of the wider adult world around her develops and matures, she will branch out into a host of new experiences – an inexorable progress towards the destiny she has knowingly chosen.

Meanwhile, both she and Prince Charles combine as best they might their public with their domestic duties. Gone, it seems, are the days when royal babies and children were rarely seen or heard, and these latest royal parents have in many of their public speeches and informal conversations made it clear that they fairly dote on young Prince William. Diana cannot resist giving daily or weekly reports on her son's progress during her many brief natters with other mothers, while during their foreign tours, Prince Charles spiced at least one speech a day with gems about some of Prince William's more mischievous or amusing propensities. They both obviously take great delight in him, and have already let slip their pet name for him – Wills. He is growing sturdily, is bright-eyed, active and alert, his once reddish-blond hair turning gradually darker. He finally acquired the knack of standing on his own two feet at the age of twelve months, about the time he made transatlantic telephone communication from Kensington Palace to Canada where his parents were on tour. He managed, according to his father, "a few squeaks". Soon, no doubt, the nurseries at Kensington and at Highgrove – the country house in Gloucestershire which Charles and Diana regard as their home – will be full of the noise of the young Prince's experiments in speech under the supervision of the nanny he has already learned to call Barbara.

Until Prince William came along, Prince Andrew was the man waiting in the wings, being next after Prince Charles in line for the Throne. Recent royal history shows that circumstances can favour the accession of the second son of the sovereign, and for the first twenty-two years of his life, Prince Andrew's chances were at least as good as those of George V and George VI when they were each Duke of York. Indeed, the same title may well accrue to Prince Andrew in turn, though the Queen is thought to prefer her children to retain the style of Prince or Princess which within virtually the next generation will distinguish the children of the sovereign from all other members of the Royal Family. In all probability, it will be only if and when Prince Andrew marries that a dukedom will be conferred upon him so that his wife – who, if she is a commoner, will strictly not be entitled to put "Princess" before her own name – can take what will then be Prince Andrew's subsidiary title, and become a Duchess.

The safe birth of Prince William will almost certainly have been a relief to Prince Andrew in particular, leaving him freer to concentrate on his chosen career in the Royal Navy. He joined up as a cadet, or "snottie", in August 1979 and signed up for twelve years on his graduation, or passing out, six months later. The prospect of sailing round the world as a naval officer clearly appealed to his outgoing nature, but little could he have guessed that within three years he would be preparing to go to war – a controversial and highly emotive war – to retrieve the Falkland Islands from Argentinian occupation. As a sublieutenant on *HMS Invincible*, he flew Sea King helicopters on reconnaissance and rescue missions, and even acted as decoy for the lethal Exocet missiles which proved vital to the Argentinian effort. When he returned he was a changed man, having learned the value of life after so many potential brushes with death, the value of camaraderie after many moments of being "very much on your own", and the value of freedom after hearing the experiences of those who for four indescribable months had suddenly and unexpectedly been deprived of it. He was almost immediately promoted to first pilot, taking full command of his helicopter, and a year later started a seven-month advanced training course in Lynx helicopters. During this time, he was promoted to lieutenant, and lived in the officers' mess at *HMS Osprey*, Portland.

In that time he gained a reputation as a fun-loving prince, a ladies' man whose activities lurched between his duties in the Navy and his much publicised love-life. Like his brother before him, he enjoyed the company of a regular succession of girlfriends, though none has proved as enduring or indeed as mysterious as the celebrated Koo Stark. His first known excursion with her was also the most publicised – a two-week holiday based at Princess Margaret's island home in Mustique.

After a mighty Press invasion of his privacy prompted him to return to London somewhat earlier that he may have anticipated, he and Koo Stark continued to see each other at irregular intervals and, according to those who claimed to be well informed, at a variety of venues. Unable to control the indiscretions of other members of his holiday party, the Prince kept a low profile and has never been photographed with Miss Stark since. He has learned the hard way that royal friendships of this sort are just as newsworthy whether you are first or third in line of succession to the Throne. A further misfortune befell when he was set up by a model, Vicky Hodge, for beach party photographs with her female friends during his shore leave in Barbados, and a change of detectives, coincidental though Buckingham Palace insisted it was, fuelled rumours that Prince Andrew had compounded his own misjudgement by a violent argument with his personal bodyguard.

These escapades have understandably coloured Prince Andrew's public image, and many people have expressed their concern at his immodest behaviour. On the other hand, others have praised him for the way in which he has seized life's opportunities with both hands, and enjoyed his fun while he can. "Nice one, Andy", shouted a group of airport workers as he returned from Mustique to London's Heathrow. Although the Press will not willingly leave him alone until he has found a wife and conformed to the ideal royal stereotype, the current speculation over his activities will eventually die down, even if people will continue to imagine that he has a girl in every port. His early nickname of Randy Andy has been hard to shake off, though it is interesting to note that it was only applied while he was in the legitimate presence of girls – at school or at college – whereas now that he is fairly openly going out with them, everyone seems to be calling him Prince Andrew again.

Perhaps that is because he is becoming slightly more 'respectable'. His naval career is well into its fifth year, and the rate of his promotions indicates that it will be a satisfying and successful occupation for him. He is already beginning to take on a few public duties and responsibilities, for which he was allocated a Private Secretary, Squadron Leader Adam Wise, in September 1983. Andrew's physique and youthful good looks – Prince Charles once called him "the one with the Robert Redford looks" – are both beginning to thicken into at least a suggestion of the heavy, squarish form of his Hanoverian ancestors. In an era when life's landmarks and achievements appear to be reached at ever earlier ages, the approach of his mid-twenties must tend to make him seem a little old for the Randy Andy image. For all his energy, determination and competitiveness, the signs are that he is beginning to settle down. That will at least please the Queen – not just as a mother, but as someone who has had to deal with some of the unedifying consequences of Prince Andrew's adventures. She was far away in Australia when the Koo Stark story broke, and in the middle of her Western Atlantic tour when the *Sun* began to publish articles alleging some doubtful behaviour by Prince Andrew at Buckingham Palace. On each occasion, she has had urgently to consider what action to take while at the same time concealing her anxiety for the benefit of those she had come to visit.

The Queen will relish the likelihood that Prince Edward will not pose the same problems. He has always been the quietest of her four children, less forthcoming as a schoolboy even than Prince Charles was, and anxious even now in his twenties to avoid publicity. Recent events have made him even more averse to it: a disappointing set of 'A' level results was held up to public notice almost as disparagingly as if he had failed in all three subjects, and the manner in which he was admitted to Jesus College Cambridge in spite of his indifferent grades unleashed a storm of protest both inside the College and out. Then he went to New Zealand, to spend two terms as a housemaster at Wanganui Collegiate, under an exchange scheme with his old school Gordonstoun. Another wave of public interest engulfed him. One tenacious British photographer travelled to New Zealand on spec, and asked whether he might take pictures of him in his classroom. Prince Edward refused, but eventually had to agree as a reasonable alternative to being pestered day after day. As he said to another photographer who followed him on one of his skiing holidays, "You're going to take my photograph anyway, so you may as well photograph me looking my best". His revenge, such as it is, takes the form of a motto on a drinking mug which he keeps on a cluttered desk in his room at Buckingham Palace: "Old photographers never die; they just go out of focus".

As the latest of the royal children to emerge from his teens, Prince Edward is very much an unknown quantity. The serious academic bent which has given him the reputation of being the brainiest of the Queen's children and which has prompted him to study archaeology, anthropology and probably history at university accounts for only one of his facets. He is physically active, and participated in a heavy schedule of jogging and cross-country running while at Wanganui. He has for many years enjoyed sailing and windsurfing, visiting Cowes each August with Prince Philip in order to keep his hand in during the prestigious Cowes Regatta. He can ski well, and goes water-skiing or surfing when, rarely, the opportunity presents itself. He is a keen horseman, and is frequently seen riding at Balmoral or Sandringham, as well as at the Badminton Horse Trials – though not competitively. He seems to have the taste for endurance too: while in New Zealand, he ventured to the South Pole for three weeks, visiting outposts used by Shackleton and Scott over seventy years earlier, living in igloos, exploring glaciers and becoming a member of the world's most southerly skiing club at Scott Base. When he returned to Britain he joined, as his brothers had done before him, the Royal Marine Commando course at Lympstone. "His feet won't touch the ground", one officer promised. They didn't, but Edward grinned, bore it and survived. Small wonder that he found teaching at Wanganui a little on the tame side.

He has not yet begun his prospective life's round of royal engagements, though he now shares Prince Andrew's Private Secretary as the amount of paperwork associated with his position grows. And if one bears in mind that Prince Charles was nineteen when he undertook his first solo public engagement, Princess Anne eighteen and Prince Andrew twenty-one, it is clear that the day cannot be far distant when Prince Edward's university career is at least occasionally interrupted by, or his vacations peppered with, official duties. He has yet to go on tour with the Queen and Prince Philip as did Prince Charles and Princess Anne in 1970, and Prince Andrew in 1978. His first public speech, his first public appointment, his first royal honour all await him. Meanwhile his Civil List allowance of £20,000 a year is being saved up and invested against the time when he will require it to fund a regular programme of service in support of the Crown.

One member of the Royal Family who knows most about service is the lady who has now completed over sixty years of it on behalf of four sovereigns. In April 1983, the Queen Mother passed the diamond anniversary of her marriage, and thus of her entry into the Royal Family as wife of the then Duke of York. As Duchess of York, she graced the latter half of King George V's reign, and the short reign of his eldest son King Edward VIII. When, on his abdication, the Crown passed to her husband, she set to work restoring the respect and credibility which the monarchy had lately lost, and helped to bring it unscathed, more admired than ever, through a tumultuous war. When peace finally came, the decline in George VI's health put personal and official burdens on his wife which she bore without a public hint of her distress. When he died, she set about reorganising her life to suit the new circumstances in which her daughter was now a popular, not to say somewhat adulated, Head of State.

The Queen Mother's contribution to the life and work of the Royal Family in the last thirty years is not like that of most of its other members. These days, you cannot qualify it by reference to the number of her public engagements, because since her early seventies she has reduced these to no more than 150 per year, and as she approaches her mid-eighties, the count now falls below a hundred. Nor can it be quantified on account of the distances she travels, since by far the majority of her duties are performed in and around London. Foreign trips in particular are now a rarity. She is content to leave the glitter and spectacle associated with being royal very much to younger members of the family. Nevertheless, out-and-out republicans apart, any member of the public will readily agree that the Royal Family, and the monarchy, would be the poorer without her.

Decorative she certainly is, with her ultra-feminine wardrobe of pinks, greens and creams, not to mention her favourite powder blue. World famous too, is that vast array of fluffy, flowery, feathered hats which softens a face that in reality needs no softening. She is distinctive as well, with that "curious, sideways lilt" as one observer remarked, the stilted, jerky wave of the white-gloved hand, the head cheerfully cocked to one side as her legendary smile broadens across her face. Above all, she is sociable. One of Britain's most outgoing octogenarians, she is everything to everybody. She seems to be as much at home inspecting vivid tattoos on a rocker's arm or the studs on his leather jacket, as conversing with the Dean of St Paul's. She enjoys the mud and biting wind of Cheltenham on Gold Cup Day every bit as much as being thoroughly regal at State banquets. She will as soon throw on an old mac and pop round the cottages on the Sandringham estate to drop in on old retainers as she will attend a Mayoral luncheon at London's Guildhall. For twenty-five years she was Chancellor of London University, and when she retired, its students, then only a quarter of her age, presented her with a scroll which praised her services and ended, "Love and kisses". A whole nation rejoiced on her eightieth birthday and even Willie Hamilton, arch-critic of royalty and the monarchy's thorn in the flesh, admitted, "For a fleeting moment my hatchet is buried, my venom dissipated".

Although, since her widowhood, the Queen Mother has been ever present to give advice, stand in or help out generally, she has not emulated some previous Queen Dowagers by attempting to keep the stage. During her daughter's reign, for instance, she has never been present at the State Opening of Parliament, nor has she attended the welcoming by the Queen of a State visitor onto British soil. Even on Remembrance Sunday, her wreath to the fallen is placed for her by her Comptroller while she watches from a balcony above, well away from the centre of attention. There are, she realises, some functions which fall exclusively within the Sovereign's prerogative, and the Queen Mother has never had any intention of muscling in. At the same time, she is regularly appointed as a Counsellor of State, performing, in conjunction with Prince Charles, Princess Anne or Princess Margaret, those duties which the Queen is unable to carry out in London owing to absence abroad. And when Lady Diana Spencer needed temporary accommodation between her engagement and her marriage, it was the Queen Mother who provided it at Clarence House.

She has by any standards an enviable life style. As a former Queen Consort, she enjoys an annual Civil List allowance of over £300,000, which enables her to keep a large staff on hand to run the administration at Clarence House, her official London residence and headquarters just a stone's throw from Buckingham Palace itself. She has three other residences. Her favourite is the pink and white Royal Lodge in the grounds of Windsor Castle, first occupied in the early 1930s after she and her husband rescued it from decades of neglect. It has always served as a weekend and holiday retreat when the Queen Mother is based in London. Then there is Birkhall, the delightful Deeside dower house on the Balmoral estate, which offers her a summer haven close to her family, and from which she used until quite recently to fish thigh-deep for salmon. Finally, the Castle of Mey – another former derelict – purchased, restored and furnished as a crusade against not only its imminent decay but also the emptiness and despair of her early widowhood. Today, she visits it once or twice a year, and it is proudly hailed as Britain's most northerly castle.

With the number of her duties diminishing, even though ever so slightly, the Queen Mother maintains annual contact with some of her favourite people and events. Shamrocks on St Patrick's Day are a must – every 17th March she visits one or other barracks where the Irish Guards are quartered to deliver the standard ration of emblems to her regiment. She was, some irreverently say, founded in the same year as they were – 1900! The Chelsea Flower Show in May – well, her presence there goes without saying. She is a gardener and always has been, and appreciates excellence wherever it is to be found. As such, she has been Patron of the London Gardens Association for over thirty years, and still takes her annual constitutional round prize-winning back gardens in all parts of the capital.

Of all her many interests, National Hunt racing is undoubtedly the best known. Her career as an owner has lasted thirty-five years and brought her over three hundred winners. She will still pay informal private visits to racecourses all over the country, especially if her own horses are running, and the Cheltenham Festival every March is an annual pilgrimage for her. On these occasions, as during the Badminton Horse Trials the following month, she stays at Badminton House as a guest of the Duke and Duchess of Beaufort. If the Queen Mother's knowledge of the finer points of breeding and form are not as computer-like as the Queen's, it is not for the want of trying. When she is not at the races herself, she keeps in touch with events at all daily meetings either by watching television or more usually by use of the "blower" – a direct link telephone system she had installed in Clarence House many years ago.

In the establishment-knocking days of the sixties, both she and the Queen were held up to some criticism for having no appreciable interest in the Arts. That has since proved an unfair assessment, particularly in respect of the Queen Mother. She has in her time acquired several valuable paintings for the Royal Collection; during the war she commissioned a set of paintings of Windsor Castle by John Piper, as artistic keepsakes in case the Castle should be destroyed by enemy action; and she has herself accumulated a very fine set of Chelsea porcelain. Like the Queen, she lends many of her paintings and *objets d'art* to art galleries and special exhibitions both at home and abroad. She is also an informed devotee of the theatre: she often visits theatres in London and Windsor privately, and has impressed theatrical friends, from Noël Coward to Peter Hall, with her prodigious and up-to-date knowledge. The Queen Mother is also an accomplished pianist and a lover of classical music. Many official photographs of her as Queen showed her at the piano, and during the war she used to attend the lunch-time piano recitals and concerts given by the National Gallery. She is an annual visitor at the King's Lynn Festival, where she used to take Prince Charles in his early youth and from which he acquired his own lifelong love of classical music.

For all her association with the gentilities of life, the Queen Mother is still surprisingly forward-looking, and rarely put off by aspects of modern-day existence. She almost puts her two daughters to shame by her consistent use of the helicopter – a favourite form of transport on official engagements for over two decades, despite the technical hitch which involved her in an emergency landing in 1982. The following year she paid a two-day visit to Northern Ireland, able under strict security to relax thoroughly and enjoy journeying to and fro and meeting people as naturally as if it were in her own back garden. She visited Brixton the same year, in spite of the recent racial tension which had seen much of the area engulfed in flames and riots. She found time to stop and listen to a street calypso band, and some people swore they noticed her swaying her hips to the rhythm of the music!

The Queen Mother has of late suffered a spate of minor ailments – sundry colds, a leg ulcer, and the consequences of the famous salmon bone which lodged in her throat recently – all of which might indicate to her that advantage might well be taken of the excuse to bow out of public life gracefully. But there is no sign of that yet. Ten years ago, Willie Hamilton referred to her disparagingly as "an old lady". That seems as inappropriate now as it did then. And, as one who passed on to her daughters the message, "Work is the rent you pay for life", the Queen Mother is up to date on her payments, and clearly expects no discounts in the future.

"Princesses", said Princess Anne once, "are getting a bit short on the market". She was talking about the European scene as it happens but it is also a sobering thought that princesses, so born in Britain, are few and far between. Princess Anne, Princess Margaret and Princess Alexandra are the only ladies, apart from the Queen, born to the purple, and it is interesting, if not a little perverse, that the two former, who are also the two senior royal princesses, are also the two most controversial. Normally, controversy in or about the Royal Family is reckoned to be a bad thing, and in the sense that it may invite contempt or unhealthy curiosity, it is clearly to be avoided. But if the speculation and sensation in the case of Princess Anne and Princess Margaret have done any good at all, it is that they have provided timely reminders that members of the Royal Family are at least human – a simple truth which seems all too frequently in the past to have been overlooked.

The similarities between them are manifold. Both Princesses were blessed, if that is the right word in the context of their comparatively restricting circumstances, with a straightforward, no-nonsense approach to life and an outspoken, unbiddable and sometimes ferociously uncompromising attitude to their existence. Both of them lived and were brought up in the shadow of elder siblings, Princess Anne having endured the additional psychological wound of being displaced in the line of succession by two subsequently-born brothers. Both princesses were, in their time, next but one in line of succession to the Throne, and thus enjoyed – and that is almost certainly the correct term – a long period during adolescence and early adulthood of public interest, most of which enhanced their respective standings as the media portrayed them as the superstars of their day. A mass of official photographs charted the birthdays of each, and their activities were relentlessly pursued under implicit official encouragement to project them into public life. Both princesses have their consuming passions – horses for Anne, and Arts and a gregarious social life for Margaret. And both have in their time come to grief with the public; one through her words and temperament, and the other through her actions and her unhappy marital history.

In the latter respect, they certainly differ. Princess Margaret's affairs of the heart, which first reached public ears in 1953 when her affection for Group Captain Peter Townsend became known, have travelled through the controversy surrounding her renunciation of him, the initial happiness of her marriage to Lord Snowdon, the misery of separation and divorce, and the squalor of the Press' pursuit of her friendship with Roddy Llewellyn. They have come to rest in loneliness, born not so much of the lack of a male escort as of the knowledge that the threat of publicity makes it impossible for her to enjoy a private, close relationship with the opposite sex. Princess Anne by contrast married comparatively early, and clearly for a love founded strongly upon a mutual interest in horses. Her marriage to Captain Mark Phillips, now over ten years old, has been fulfilling, highly successful and above all comparatively private. Public curiosity has been satisfied since the couple have produced two handsome children who now follow their parents on their country-wide travels to horse trials and events, and make pleasant mischief while royal backs are turned.

Princess Margaret has become accustomed to risking her privacy as an inevitable consequence of the enviable social life she leads. Unlike her niece, who has only ever been to nightclubs a couple of times in her life, who has to be positively dragged to parties, and who admits to not being "much enamoured of London", Princess Margaret, one of the most extrovert in the family, is also its greatest party-goer and socialite. She has a phenomenal interest in the Arts – particularly ballet, opera and the theatre – and her official engagements tend to reflect these inclinations more closely than with any other member of the family. Like her mother, she is an accomplished pianist, and her superb gift of mimicry makes her a great entertainer at any of the numerous private parties to which she is invited. Some say that her impersonation of Mae West is second to none.

Her range of close friends is enormous. Many of them are from the world of showbusiness and the Arts – the late Peter Sellers was one; Rudolph Nureyev, the Russian ballet dancer who defected to the West in the mid-1960s, is another. Others boast a more aristocratic upbringing, and of these none has been a greater or more consistent friend than Colin Tennant, the heir of Lord Glenconner. It was Tennant who gave Princess Margaret her elegant holiday home *Les Jolies Eaux* on the island of Mustique as a wedding present. And it is to that residence that, once or twice a year – usually in February and November – she flies with a small party of staff and friends to spend two or three weeks in the Caribbean sunshine. In addition, she frequently spends a week or ten days in the Mediterranean at the height of summer. Until a few years ago, she was a regular guest of another close friend, the Aga Khan, in Sardinia. More recently she has visited Northern Italy and was, for instance, enjoying a week in and around Venice at the time of Prince William's christening in August 1982.

Princess Anne manages to guard her privacy more circumspectly. Outside her official engagements, she has to suffer the curiosity of the Press and people only at the numerous equestrian events she attends, though even here she is nowadays left alone for much longer than she used to be. Her country home – something Princess Margaret lacks – is her haven, a place where she can relax with her family after a week in which she has been apart from them. For, with young Peter Phillips a pupil at Minchinhampton Blue Boys' School, his sister Zara still a toddler, and their father Captain Mark Phillips permanently busy running the estates at Gatcombe Park, there is little opportunity during a normal week for Princess Anne to be with them. Her duties take her to all parts of the United Kingdom: she spends several days a year carrying out official engagements in Scotland, many of them during August or September when she is based at Balmoral. She once said that, as far as holidays were concerned, "a week or two at Balmoral or ten days at Sandringham is the nearest we get". In respect of the public engagements she undertakes during the so-called royal holiday at Balmoral, this is certainly true. With Captain Phillips now invariably at Gatcombe supervising the harvest, Princess Anne's visit to Balmoral is spent more for the benefit of the Scots, or for the purpose of allowing the Queen to see her Phillips grandchildren for longer than usual, than in the search of a true family holiday.

Captain Phillips' preoccupation with his farming activities to the apparent exclusion of his wife has recently cast doubts upon the stability of their marriage, and at one point the suspicion of its imminent breakdown became difficult to throw off. It was indeed odd that no-one had ever taken Captain Phillips very seriously when he first attended a nine-month farm management course at the Royal College of Agriculture at Cirencester, whereas the subsequent earnestness of his purpose – the efficient running of Gatcombe under his qualified management – became mistaken for apathy towards his wife and family. The same illogical results have followed his reluctance to attend royal engagements with Princess Anne. He admits that formal or indeed public duties of this kind are not his scene, which is why he prefers not to take part. No doubt his critics would call him a sponger if he did. As it is, his persistent absences from his wife's side in public lead to the periodic speculation that attends all royal married couples at some time or other – that separation or divorce is not far distant.

Both Princess Anne and Princess Margaret have remained fairly close to the bottom of many so-called popularity polls organised or commissioned by British newspapers or magazines. In this sense, the British monarchy is very much like a soap opera in which it becomes fashionable to fête certain participants as heroes and to despise others equally as villains. There is no doubt that in Princess Margaret's case her villainous stereotype is due to a private life so highly publicised as one of extravagance and luxury that the gossip writers keep daily tabs on her activities and publish the more salacious titbits, however irrelevant they may be.

By contrast, Princess Anne owes much of the disfavour surrounding her to the (comparatively occasional) examples of abrupt behaviour or blunt words which follow a brush with unwelcome company. Photographers eager to picture her as she falls from horses or is catapulted by them into water splashes are as likely to be told to "naff off" – or even worse – as is the reporter who accompanies a personal question with a microphone thrust in her face. She has been seen rather sulkily shrugging away the hand of an oversolicitous official; she has been known to walk past lines of patient children without so much as a word to them; she lost many friends when, during her visit to the United States, she reacted rather snappily to the news of Prince William's birth as it was informally relayed to her by a local reporter. Official explanations for all such examples of surly behaviour are usually hastily given, but of course it is the image that lasts, and Princess Anne has paid dearly for her indiscretions. Her exhaustive work for Riding for the Disabled and the Save the Children Fund have helped to restore her reputation as a hard-working Princess, and her 1982 tour of Save the Children Fund projects in nine African and Middle East countries completely turned public opinion back in her favour. On this occasion she was seen to be an active and concerned woman, sometimes fearless for her own safety, having a taste for adventure and not a little natural sympathy for the less fortunate. It was the sort of transition that makes it clear that however much the Royal Family may dislike the idea of 'image', it is an inescapable fact of life for any public figure.

For Princess Margaret, the task of reinstating herself in the eyes of the public has not been easy. Two books have recently been published about her, one by a tabloid gossip writer who claimed she had seen and approved much of the book; the other written at her own behest by a friend and admirer, Christopher Warwick. Neither did very much to further her cause: the former was lambasted publicly by her friends for its inaccuracies; the latter was suspected, on account of an honest acknowledgement of the Princess' own hand in it, of being too partial by half.

Certainly many former critics have been pleasantly surprised by the way in which Princess Margaret has slimmed since the days when they accused her of gross self-indulgence, and by the greater discretion with which she has enjoyed her legitimate right to private life of late. "Disobedience is my joy", she is said to have told Jean Cocteau, and the devil-may-care attitude with which she once insisted on pursuing her lawful avocations untarnished by any hint of hypocrisy or concealment was patently not to the public's liking. It is incontrovertible that her contribution to public life has been as creditable as that of most other members of the Royal Family, bearing in mind the size of her annual allowance. It is therefore somewhat unfair that, while she takes her leisure in the full glare of publicity, she works very much in the shadow of the more spectacular doings of the Queen, the Princess of Wales and Princess Anne.

For it is a fact that few of her official duties these days command much public attention. She has for thirty years served as Patron of the National Society for the Prevention of Cruelty to Children, yet when the Society presented her with a silver goblet to commemorate those thirty years, the event went pretty well unmarked by the Press. The Princess has been an equally long-standing President of the Girl Guides Association, a supporter of the Victoria League and a frequent guest of honour at gala performances where her very presence raises funds for appeals for orchestras, opera houses and the Royal Ballet. Yet public recognition is sparse and unenthusiastic. The experience of one occasion recently, however, may give her hope. On her way to a dinner-dance at London's Dorchester Hotel, she walked through a crowd of spectators, one of whom shouted out – spontaneously it seemed – "God save our Royal Family!" Visibly nonplussed, Princess Margaret must nevertheless have thought it the nicest unsought compliment that had been paid to her after years of public brickbats. Perhaps, like Princess Anne's, her star is once again in the ascendant.

The late Duke of Gloucester died in 1974 after a stroke which left him chair-bound for six years. His widow, Princess Alice, is now in her eighties, and it was the landmark of her eightieth birthday which led her to the decision that she must reduce the number of her engagements and retire "with regret but also with relief" from public life. The sentiment is entirely understandable. Though not by nature shy, she has always been modest and averse to the risk of the false glamour that public exposure can entail. When her husband suffered his stroke, she had to assume the burden of his duties as well as her own, since her elder son Prince William was fully occupied as a Civil Servant in the Commonwealth Relations Office. Princess Alice endured the successive emotional shocks of Prince William's sudden and tragic death in 1972, when his light aircraft crashed at the beginning of an air race near Wolverhampton, and the late Duke's much slower and more distressing decline until his death less than two years later. Since then, her younger son, the present Duke of Gloucester, and his wife have assimilated the round of public duties they never expected to inherit, to the point where Princess Alice has clearly felt able to bow out.

It is a graceful and gradual exit, though accomplished with some difficulty. She is well aware of the disappointment that a royal refusal brings in its wake, and has for some time felt morally bound, even though against her better judgement, to attend those functions which threaten to flop through her absence. But she also freely recognises that she is "failing in sight and limbs" and that, being a country woman at heart, the peaceful delights of house and garden at Barnwell, the family manor in Northamptonshire, are now due to her in full measure.

Unsuspecting of his own destiny, the Duke of Gloucester married at a time when he fully expected to be spending his life as a partner in the family farming concern, as a qualified architect, and as an enthusiastic amateur photographer. While his father and brother were still alive, he and his Danish-born wife sought a London retreat – some say they were thinking of settling on the Isle of

Dogs – as a means of staying well out of the public eye. The Duke had already set himself up in partnership as an architectural consultant, and had produced a couple of photographic essays under the unassuming pen name, Richard Gloucester. Then he inherited his brother's share of the farming partnership at Barnwell as well as the inevitable legacy of public duty.

Today, the Duke's public engagements strongly reflect his major interests. As a farmer he attends agricultural shows throughout the country – in particular the Royal Show at Stoneleigh and the East of England Show at Peterborough, just a few miles from Barnwell. He attends meetings and conferences of the Royal Smithfield Club, and in the course of any one year visits farming projects of all types – from pig units to the development of combine harvesters, from farming community experiments to farm training schemes. As an architect with a passion for the preservation of the best in old buildings, he has accepted presidential positions in heritage bodies such as the Victorian Society, the Heritage of London Trust, and the Building Conservation Trust. The Duke is keenly interested in history, and is an admirer of his ancestor Prince Albert as well as of his famous namesake, the Richard Duke of Gloucester who later became Richard III. That particular fascination came to fruition in 1983, the 500th anniversary of the Yorkist King's accession. The Duke attended a quincentenary dinner and a lecture in London, carried out a series of engagements in Yorkshire in connection with the anniversary, and gave interviews to the Press as part of the growing campaign to clarify the facts surrounding Richard III's notoriety, and hopefully to clear his name.

He shares a hefty programme of other engagements with his wife, the former Birgitte van Deurs who, until her engagement, worked with the Danish Embassy in London. Like her husband and parents-in-law, she is and always has been thoroughly unassuming. She is perfectly content to fulfil her public duties without attracting instant publicity and expects her brief periods of leisure – she is a good skier and the Duke and Duchess frequently take a skiing holiday in February – to be treated likewise. She has chosen the three dozen or so public positions she holds carefully, and with a distinct medical emphasis. She shares the Duke's commitment to the Order of St John, and once worked part-time in its Ambulance Brigade. She also spent some time as a student nurse at the Great Ormond Street Hospital for Sick Children, and many of her duties today show her continuing interest in the care of children. Her own children – she has suffered several miscarriages in the process of producing a family of three – are her pride and joy. She and the Duke agreed that, instead of being educated from home in Northamptonshire, they should accompany their parents from Barnwell to London each week and attend school there. In addition to normal classes, their second child, Lady Davina Windsor, attends special sessions at a London dyslexia centre.

In the same way that Princess Alice deputised for her husband in the late 1960s and early 1970s, the present Duke of Kent has found himself frequently covering for his wife in recent years. The marriage of the Duke to the former Miss Katharine Worsley, the daughter of a Yorkshire landowner, in 1961 has undergone considerable pressure owing to the Duchess' indifferent health lately. For the first fifteen years, all went ideally: two early children were followed by a late addition in 1970, but trouble began with the Duchess' fourth pregnancy in 1977. The risks of child-bearing at the age of 45 proved all too evident, and her miscarriage that October began a chapter of medical and psychiatric misfortunes. The successive removal of her gall bladder and an ovarian cyst, and treatment for a slipped disc and for an obstruction in the gall bladder duct involved several spells in hospital, while two months after the death of her mother in 1979, the Duchess underwent a long period of treatment for mental strain.

They have proved hard times indeed for a couple who had succeeded in keeping their domestic lives well and truly apart from their inescapable public role, and whose children were brought up almost unnoticed by the media. The Duchess blazed a trail which has since been well worn by the Gloucesters, Phillipses and Waleses, when she decided to have her third child, Lord Nicholas Windsor, born in hospital, and it was she personally who first presented him to the press cameras on leaving the hospital a few days later. The same fundamental simplicity is present in all her attitudes and those of her husband, a man brought up in a household which by no means matched the circumstances of many of his royal cousins. Indeed, in 1972 the financial strain of maintaining the family home in Buckinghamshire proved to be too much. The house had to be sold, and the Duke and his family moved to Anmer House, a residence on the Sandringham estate provided by the Queen.

That change of circumstances occurred shortly after the Duke of Kent left the Army, which he had always hoped to make his career. He had already spent time commanding a unit in Northern Ireland shortly after the present troubles broke out, but was recalled early on grounds of security. He now maintains his link with the services mainly through honorary rank, which includes that of Colonel of the Scots Guards. He is a personal *aide-de-camp* to the Queen, who promoted him to supernumerary Major General on her official birthday in 1983. In his civilian capacity, the prime charges on his time are the presidency of the Royal National Lifeboat Institution, a position which takes him and the Duchess all over the country to name and launch lifeboats and to encourage appeals; and British exports, in support of which he makes frequent trips abroad, though only occasionally accompanied by his wife. In private life he is an enthusiastic photographer – he once issued a series of his pictures of his daughter Lady Helen Windsor as official photographs to mark her fourteenth birthday – and well practised at skiing, a sport in which the Duchess and their two younger children also participate.

The Duchess of Kent's public service encompasses a wide range of charitable work, and she seems most at home in the comparatively undemanding presence of children. Indeed, until the Princess of Wales came along, it was the Duchess who was most regularly seen stooping to talk to children, or holding them in her arms, or chatting informally with them during visits to homes, hospitals and schools. Her genuine compassion, sharpened by her own personal experiences, made her the natural choice for the delicate mission to Mousehole to attend the memorial service for the victims of the Penlee lifeboat tragedy in January 1982. Her concern on such occasions is not merely perfunctory. Some years ago, she went into training with the Samaritans – an entirely voluntary decision unconnected with her public engagements, yet undoubtedly prompted by her very real sympathy for human problems in all walks of life.

In 1968, the Duke succeeded his mother Princess Marina as President of the All England Lawn Tennis Association, and he and the Duchess attend the championships during many days of Wimbledon fortnight each year, presenting the prizes at the end of the competition. The Duchess' interest is very strong, and in the late 1970s she prompted the moves by which the parents of the women's champion Martina Navratilova were ultimately allowed to leave Czechoslovakia and see their daughter take the title. The Duchess' other great passion is music: it features frequently in her private as well as her public life. She is a member of the Bach Choir, and as such has sung in performances all over the country. The fact that it was with the Bach Choir that she was seen for the first time after a long recuperation from an operation in May 1983 gave currency to the impression that singing has been of great therapeutic value to her.

The Duke of Kent's only brother, Prince Michael, enjoyed relative obscurity as a member of the Royal Family when he was an officer in the Royal Hussars. His marriage in 1978 changed all that: it was a potentially controversial one, since his bride was a Catholic and a divorcée, though in the event Prince Michael was too far down the line of succession for the issue to become one of national or constitutional importance. As it was, he simply renounced his claim to the Throne, and in a couple of quiet ceremonies in Vienna married the woman who is now universally admired as Princess Michael. Formerly Baroness Marie Christine von Reibnitz, she had married an English banker Thomas Troubridge, from whom she obtained a divorce in 1977. At first, the Roman Catholic Church refused to sanction her marriage to Prince Michael while she refused an assurance that any children would be brought up as Catholics. The Vatican has since relented, and a formal blessing was granted in July 1983 in a ceremony at Westminster Cathedral. The Michaels have two delightful children, Lord Frederick and Lady Gabriella Windsor – Freddie and Ella – and a country home at Nether Lyppiatt in Gloucestershire, part of the "royal triangle" which also includes Highgrove and Gatcombe.

As junior male representative of the Kent family, Prince Michael is not required to carry out official engagements, does not receive any public funds, and neither his activities nor those of his wife warrant a mention in the Court Circular. There are just occasional exceptions – they represented the Queen at the independence celebrations for Belize in 1981, and Princess Michael undertook engagements on behalf of the Queen Mother during her convalescence from an operation in November 1982. Yet, despite the lack of official recognition, in the few years since their marriage, they have proved as popular as any junior ranking members of the Royal Family, and indeed more popular at times than one or two more senior ranking members. Between them, they undertake well over a hundred engagements a year, ranging over a fairly wide spectrum. Princess Michael attends Women of the Year luncheons, visits the Ideal Home Exhibition, opens art exhibitions and attends charity auctions, for instance, while her husband tends to indulge his particular forte – the motor car – in connection with his duties. His engagements as President of the Institute of Motor Industries account for far more than any other single position he holds. His fascination for cars dates from his teens; he has driven in several RAC rallies – the famous London to Brighton veteran car runs – has taken part in the World Cup Rally to Mexico, has passed the British School of Motoring's high speed course of driving, and has become a member of the Institute of Advanced Motorists.

Both he and Princess Michael have several sporting interests in common. They frequently go riding in Hyde Park early in the morning, making their way from their apartments in Kensington Palace, their London headquarters. While in Gloucestershire, they join one or other of the local hunt meetings, and Princess Michael is proving to be an adept, if not yet particularly successful rider, at local point-to-point meetings. Both the Prince and Princess enjoy yachting, and although neither owns a yacht, the British challenger for the America's Cup gave them sufficient opportunity to sail recently. Having named *Victory '83* and inspected the yacht several times, the Prince and Princess visited the Bahamas to watch her progress during trials, then attended some of the actual racing off Newport, Rhode Island. More recently, and less confidently, the couple have tried their hand at ballooning. Their instructor Giles Bellew thought that Princess Michael showed more liking for the sport than her husband, but time alone will tell whether it will become a royal favourite.

Princess Michael is now nearing completion of her biography of Queen Elizabeth of Bohemia – a daughter of James I – which she has been researching in Holland, Austria and Czechoslovakia for over three years. The project has taken her longer than originally anticipated, partly because of an unexpectedly high increase in the number of public duties in the last two years, and partly because of her own insistence that her work should not cut across her responsibilities as a mother more than is absolutely necessary. Consequently she sees a great deal of her children, especially first thing in the morning and last thing at night, which she regards as essential. She has instilled in them a great love of animals, and rabbits, dogs, goats and horses now abound at Nether Lyppiatt. No species is more popular, however, than the Oriental cats the Princess herself adores. She was heartbroken when one of her Burmese cats was found dead in a nearby timberyard recently, and quickly acquired two more to replace it.

It is widely held that Princess Michael revels in being royal, though that is a characteristic that her sister-in-law Princess Alexandra is less willing to entertain as part of her own make-up. "I am first of all a human being", she once said, "and secondly a member of the Royal Family". It is a sentiment that cuts both ways. In one sense it means that she can feel free to be herself. She is now twenty-first in line of succession to the Throne, and the fact that she has never been higher than the sixth place she was in at her birth has meant that she has always been able to forget about the more rarified heights of royal existence and remain delightfully natural at all times. "If it's all too pompous, I always want to laugh", she once admitted, and certainly the people she has met have been struck by her complete informality. An unobtrusive upbringing, and an education which for a royal princess was then novel in its relative normality, have left Princess Alexandra with none of the inhibitions which can often clutter the life style of those of sterner schooling.

In another sense, her statement indicates her personal insistence upon her rights as a human being, including that of privacy when not on public duty. "I have the nicest private life of any of us", she is said to have boasted, and that is a right she has guarded jealously. She seeks no greater privilege than is necessary for one who has a public persona and public responsibilities, but at the end of the day, enough is enough. It may seem a dull sort of attitude when you consider some of the triumphant publicity other members of the Royal Family get in their amenable moments, but peace and quiet is Princess Alexandra's preferred life style, and an existence as little punctuated by the click of cameras as possible is what enables her to make her jovial, easy-going contribution to public life.

Brought up comparatively modestly by her widowed mother Princess Marina, she was also her constant companion rather after the style of the younger or only daughters of widows in Victorian times. But it didn't last forever. Though she accompanied her mother in public engagements in this country and on foreign tours from the age of sixteen, she was carrying out her own public duties at seventeen – a self-composed young lady whose presence and maturity had all the gossip-writers scanning the horizon for possible suitors. It was eight more years before she found her own, and two decades have now passed since she and the Hon Angus Ogilvy were married in Westminster Abbey. The marriage has been a supremely happy one, crowned by the birth of a son, James, in 1964, and a daughter, Marina, in 1966. It survived the shattering effect of the Lonrho affair in which Mr Ogilvy's reputation was threatened, and which impelled him to resign four dozen City directorships at a stroke.

Throughout those twenty years, the Ogilvys have lived at Thatched House Lodge, a fine, well-shielded house in Richmond Park, from which Princess Alexandra undertakes her public engagements while her husband attends to his remaining business interests including that of being a director on the board of Sotheby's. But he also accompanies Princess Alexandra on many of her evening engagements – visits to the theatre, concert halls, dinners and State occasions – and is her most frequent representative at memorial services which royal duties or protocol prevent her from attending personally. Despite the agonies of persistent back trouble, for which considerable treatment in the past has been necessary, he has proved a consistent and assiduous source of support for his wife, and an ideal family man.

Princess Alexandra's first, and longest-established public position was as Patron of the British Red Cross Society. It fitted in well with her training as a nurse in child welfare although, she confessed later, "I was always terrified of dropping a baby on its head". But her "try-anything-once" attitude has since become celebrated. Her tally of 'firsts' includes a royal ride on a London Transport bus, and another trip on a Chinese sampan. She did this during her famous visit to Hong Kong shortly before her marriage – a visit which gave her her first view – from a safe distance – of Red China, and which introduced her to Chinese cuisine. She has never looked back, and she and her family are regular customers at Chinese restaurants in and around Richmond.

While Thatched House Lodge remains Princess Alexandra's private home, she clearly experiences the same inconvenience as did the future King George VI and Queen Elizabeth when, as Duke and Duchess of York, they too lived in Richmond Park – that of being up to an hour's drive away from the centre of London. The inordinate toll in travel and police escorts this would normally entail has been reduced by the simple expedient of taking a small suite of offices at Friary Court in St James's Palace. She shares with her brother Prince Michael the dubious distinction of having one of the smallest permanent staffs, who have their work cut out making all the necessary arrangements, from start to finish, for the hundred or more engagements she undertakes each year.

When, at the end of each year's duties, the Royal Family leaves St George's Chapel Windsor after Christmas Morning service, it is Princess Alexandra and her family who are the last to emerge into public view. That is because she is the Crown's most junior ranking royal servant, but her place at the back of the crowd suits her preference for being out of the limelight. Nevertheless it is very much her day, since she was a Christmas Day baby, and combines her Christmas festivities with her birthday celebrations. The Queen throws a party for her, and for Princess Alice – also born on Christmas Day, though thirty-five years earlier – and the two royal ladies share a special birthday cake.

In many ways the ultimate illogicality of twelve months of royal activity is that, as each year draws to its close on a society which regards the maintenance of democracy as its prime concern, the Royal Family should temporarily withdraw from public life more popular and more securely based than ever. We pride ourselves on striving towards some concept of social equality, yet not only do we suffer a patently privileged body to remain at the head of our social system, but actively encourage that state of affairs. Despite the lack of clear logic in this, those who would fight for the monarchy's removal on that ground ignore the deep-seated emotional need for a system which, having outlived its original, power-based purpose, has yielded to change in such a way as to maintain and even increase its appeal. Constitutionally it is accepted that the monarchy's power is purely residual, ready for use in an emergency: as such, our only political need is for a monarch, while the family which surrounds him or her becomes superfluous. But for centuries, sovereign and family have been inseparable in the eyes of the people they serve. The social and psychological reasons behind the fact are complex and often hotly disputed, but the millions who dutifully turn out each year in the hope of the merest glimpse of one or other member of the Royal Family are living proof of it.

In Britain that social phenomenon is well over a century old, though at no time has it manifested itself more forcefully or more consistently than in the last fifty years. For over thirty of them Queen Elizabeth II has been on the Throne, presiding over a growing family which, by and large, has carried out its public duties in an exemplary and uncomplaining manner, absorbing both praise and criticism with equally receptive minds. By maintaining all that has proved popular in the past, and modifying or substituting for that which is not, the Queen and today's Royal Family have strengthened the basis on which the Crown of a thousand years is founded. If, in a rapidly changing world, it can keep the affections of its present subjects and attract those of coming generations, its own immediate future seems unshakable.

Her Majesty at the ceremony of Trooping the Colour (previous page). She has attended all the major royal weddings of her reign. Her sister, Margaret, was married in May 1960 (above); her daughter, Anne, in November 1973 (opposite, top) and her son, Charles, in July 1981 (opposite, bottom). Her own wedding portraits, from November 1947, are shown (top and right).

e Queen has reigned over Great
ain and Northern Ireland since
2. Her vitality and enjoyment of
royal duties is obvious (both
es). During the time that she has
n Sovereign, she has witnessed
mous changes: the British Empire is
more; only the Commonwealth remains.

In October 1981, during a visit to
Dunedin, New Zealand (right), the Queen
was given a photograph of the Royal
Family from July 1947, taken at the
time of her engagement to Prince
Philip. It is now customary for her to
meet her subjects in such informal
walkabouts.

Her Majesty has to attend numerous public engagements and is admirably supported by her husband, Prince Philip. She has managed to maintain a happy and contented family life despite the constant pressures of affairs of state. Wherever she goes there are crowds of well-wishers (above), showing their continued support for the monarchy.

With the Duke of Edinburgh, Her Majesty has travelled all over the Commonwealth. She is greeted as Queen by her subjects throughout the world. However, she and her husband had to part from each other (below) after a visit to Canada in April 1982. Philip gave her a swift but unprecedented public kiss at the bottom of the aircraft steps. In March, they were hosts to Sultan Qaboos of Oman (bottom). Close relations with Oman go back to the 1970s, when the Sultan was aided by British soldiers, who later helped defend his country against guerilla incursions.

The roles that the Queen undertakes are numerous. She attends the State Opening of Parliament each year (top left), seen here with Charles and Anne in November 1973, travelling in the Irish State Coach. In May 1982, she went to Westminster Abbey to install new Knights Grand Cross of the Order of the Bath (top right). Inspecting the Coldstream Guards (centre left); the Queen attending the Royal British Legion's Festival of Remembrance (above); visiting the Chelsea Pensioners (left and far left) and inspecting a detachment of the Yeomen of the Guard (right).

e Queen has travelled more
ensively than any previous
onarch. Although she is
en surrounded by cameras,
r Majesty is also a keen
otographer herself. On all
royal tours she takes a
mera with her and loses no
portunity to add another
ture to her private
lection. However, the
omy weather at the 1976
ntreal Olympics (top left),
ced her to keep the camera
shut on more than one
asion! The Queen uses a
iety of cameras, as seen
these pages, and her
rest is of course echoed
other royals, notably the
l of Lichfield and Lord
owdon.

The Queen is honoured by her subjects in all her lands. Garlands of flowers are given to her to show love and loyalty. When she visited Tuvalu, in October 1982, the people brought her to the island in a canoe, then carried her ashore on their shoulders (above). Later, she was crowned with frangipani flowers (right). Canada and Sri Lanka (opposite top) also gave floral tributes.

Diplomacy involves her in meeting many international figures. The Queen of the Netherlands' State Visit in 1974 (above left); Holland in 1958 (right); Her Majesty arriving for the State banquet given by King Khalid of Saudi Arabia in June 1981 (bottom left); hosting Commonwealth Prime Ministers at Buckingham Palace in 1977 (bottom centre); at a dinner given by the Canadian Prime Minister, Mr Trudeau (bottom right) and at a banquet during the same tour to the Canadian provinces in 1978 (opposite). Arriving at the Pipers' Ball (top right).

The Queen's visit to Tuvalu (opposite pages) in 1982, was a mixture of warmth and informality. The canoes in which she and her husband arrived, were built of a light hardwood called puka, and cost no more than £150. They were copies of those used locally for skipjack fishing, brightly painted for the occasion.

Prince Philip is arguably the most travelled man in the world, averaging 75,000 miles a year. He attends many engagements with his wife (this page) but now limits himself to some 250 – 300 a year. However, he did once travel 1,500 miles to squeeze in 30 different functions and make 15 speeches in the course of a single week.

In April 1982, the Queen and Prince Philip were in Canada and attended several official engagements as part of the handing over of the country's constitution. She welcomed guests to a State reception and banquet in Ottawa (right and top left). She was wearing a matching combination of diamond and ruby jewellery – the tiara was made up from her own collection of stones for the visit to Windsor by the President of Mexico in 1973. The Queen had previously been in Canada in 1978 and is pictured wearing a Canadian Order on her evening dress (above). In December 1982, Her Majesty attended a new production of *Peter Pan* in support of Great Ormond Street Hospital (top right). At a medal-awarding ceremony in Australia (opposite page).

The Queen is pictured at her desk at Balmoral in the summer of 1972 (top left). Only rarely do she and her husband use Balmoral Castle other than for their summer holiday, but in January 1977 they had photographs taken which were published on the 25th anniversary of her accession to the Throne (left and top right). On her 30th anniversary in 1982, they were at Sandringham (above and opposite page, top right). The Queen is very interested in the racing and breeding of horses and attends many equestrian events (opposite page). In thirty years she has not yet achieved her avowed aim, "to breed a horse that wins the Derby".

The role of monarch involves much pomp and ceremony. The balcony at Buckingham Palace has held many a royal group as shown on these pages. In June 1982, she and the rest of the Royal Family (opposite page, bottom left) witnessed and acknowledged the Royal Air Force's birthday tribute to the head of the armed forces. In this role, the Queen leads her troops on horseback on her Birthday Parade. The 1981 ceremony of Trooping the Colour was marred by an incident in the Mall when six blank shots were fired at her. She quickly recovered her composure and was all smiles on the balcony afterwards (opposite page, second from bottom).

The Queen arrived in Bahrein
on a tour of the Gulf States
in February 1979. She
entertained the Amir on board
Britannia (opposite). On the
Saudi-Arabian visit she was
greeted by King Khalid at
Riyadh airport (above) and
conferred with him (below).
In 1982, she was host to the
Sultan of Oman (below right).

Elizabeth II, gracious Sovereign Queen, is Britain's finest ambassador. Following in the wake of her many travels, trade and foreign relations improve and the esteem held for this country abroad, grows.

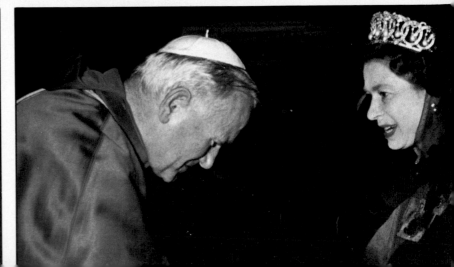

A forty-minute meeting took place on 28th May, 1982, between Pope John Paul II and the Queen (previous page – Her Majesty dressed in blue). This followed an audience with the Pope in 1980 (remaining photographs).

On these pages can be seen members of the oldest Order of Chivalry in the Kingdom: The Most Noble Order of the Garter was founded in 1348 by King Edward III and is now celebrated each St George's Day in Windsor Castle.

During 1982 the Queen had a special word for 99-year-old Dorothy Kennish in Brisbane (top). She meets some monks in Sri Lanka (above) and the families of RAF personnel (left). Opposite page: the Queen admits that she is, not particularly renowned for her green fingers, but is seen at the Chelsea Flower Show (top left) each year.

When she went to Merseyside in May 1982 (centre left), there was one group of protesters waving banners proclaiming "Reality not Royalty" and chanting slogans. Others tore down the banners and began singing the National Anthem. There was quite a fracas but the Queen, with practised aplomb, appeared not to notice.

There has always been a special relationship between Britain and the United States. The first President to stay at Windsor was Ronald Reagan, who went for a canter with the Queen in Home Park (opposite page, top left). Ever ready with a wave and a smile, Her Majesty wins the affection of millions. In Australia, she met the French singer Sacha Distel (above).

In May 1982, she followed the fortunes of her husband in the International Carriage Driving Grand Prix (top right). In June of the same year, she inspected the RAF Regiment (right) and was also seen at a Commonwealth variety performance in Brisbane (bottom left) and at the Commonwealth Games in October 1982 (bottom right).

Kandy, Sri Lanka (opposite), ceremonial umbrellas
[acc]ompanied the Queen and Prince Philip. She also
[visi]ted Tarawa (above) where she received honours in
[the] form of dried-leaf garlands and plaited cords.
[Wh]ile in Canberra she visited the War Memorial, after
[whi]ch the crowds (right) were waiting to meet her.
[At] Windsor Castle with President Reagan (top right).
[Th]e Stallion Show, Newmarket (below).

The Reagans celebrated their 31st wedding anniversary on 4th March, 1983, when the Queen held a dinner on board *Britannia* in their honour (opposite page, top left). The previous June they had visited England, arriving at Windsor to be greeted with the rousing strains of the British and American national anthems. Protocol demanded that the Queen and President Reagan should stand level with each other. At the last moment, however, Mrs Reagan stepped forward, leaving Prince Philip and Prince Charles behind (opposite page, bottom right). President Giscard d'Estaing of France visited the Queen in 1977 (right). In Qatar (top right) inspecting a guard of honour, one of her many duties as a visiting monarch.

The Queen and Queen Mother are pictured together at the 1981 Derby (above). While her mother is keen on steeplechasing, the Queen is interested in flat racing. In earlier days they jointly owned a chaser, but Her Majesty gave up her interest when the horse broke a leg and had to be destroyed. At Royal Ascot (top left, top right and centre left). She gestures expressively while talking with Princess Michael (left) at the Derby. On the morning of one of the four days of Ascot, the Royal Family have use of the course for their own private race! Prince Philip is, of course, more interested in four-in-hand carriage driving; Princess Anne likes three day eventing and Prince Charles has a penchant for polo, riding for the Maple Leaf team and Les Diables Bleus, although the press has a field-day photographing him whenever he falls off his horse.

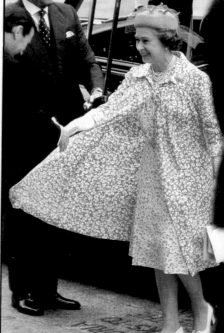

A montage of pictures of the Queen, fulfilling her many roles (previous pages). The Trooping of the Colour (these pages) is a custom going back many years. The flag itself would be carried among the soldiers on the eve of a battle so that they could recognise it as a rallying point amid the battle's smoke and slaughter. Ceremonially parading the colours of a guards battalion – embroidered with battle honours – before the sovereign, began in 1805 and has continued each year since. The Queen has made a point, throughout her reign, of leading her troops as Commander-in-Chief of the armed forces, off the parade ground and along The Mall. She rides side-saddle on a police horse that has been trained to behave placidly amid all the din of the military bands and the cheering and shouting. 1,600 officers and men from five regiments of foot-guards and two regiments of horse-guards take part.

Queen Elizabeth II heads perhaps the most stable monarchy in the world. As head of a vast Commonwealth of nations, she is uniquely placed to propound the virtues of democracy, freedom and the pursuit of individual liberty. In these days of social unrest, the durability of the Royal Family is a force for traditional values.

At the Coronation of Queen Elizabeth II in 1953 it rained. When she visited the Reagans in California there were floods and she had to spend a night in a hotel. No wonder she takes an umbrella with her!

Manchester in May 1982 (above); in July 1982 it was Scotland (below); California in March 1983 (right). Indeed, when she went to Kiribati in the South Sea Islands, a man was hired to ensure good weather.

Above all, the Queen is the head of a family in which children play a very important part. Now with the birth of Prince William (opposite page, top), Her Majesty has three grandchildren.

Opposite page: the Queen visits Merseyside (top left); Reading (top centre); Perth (top right); Adelaide Country Club (bottom left); Perth (bottom centre); at the annual parade of the Chelsea Pensioners (bottom right).

This page: on the tour of Australia and New Zealand (left); on a visit to Canada (bottom left) and to Brisbane (below), where she collected so many bunches of flowers that journalists following her had to help carry them!

In California as guest of the Reagans (previous pages). The Queen is the head of a monarchy that is the oldest secular institution in Britain. She traces her lineage back to Cerdic, who landed here in 495. Her Majesty is the head of the Royal Family; this country's constitutional monarch; head of the Church of England and of the Commonwealth, so fulfilling many roles both as Sovereign and mother.

Throughout her many years as a member of the Royal Family the Queen Mother has made a point of attending functions of state where she feels her presence is required. Among these are the annual ceremony of the Knights of the Garter (left and above), visits to the Cinque Ports (right) of which she is Lord Warden and her annual visit to the Royal British Legion's Field of Remembrance at St Margaret's Westminster.

The Queen Mother's style of dress, with its straight lines and pastel shades, has become a distinctive feature of her many appearances (these and previous pages). The birth of her three great-grandchildren, with two of whom she is pictured (facing page left) were occasions of great joy for the Queen Mother.

(Previous pages) The start of Royal Ascot is marked each year by the Royal carriage procession along the course. This popular ritual is a splendid opening to the premier occasion of the flat racing season. (These pages) It came as a surprise to nobody that Lady Diana Spencer moved into Clarence House during her engagement to the Prince of Wales. The Queen Mother, whose grace, charm and patience have become almost legendary, was chosen to educate the prospective Princess in the duties and etiquette of Royalty. Lady Diana had to learn small matters, such as stance, as well as the more important court custom, such as who to curtsey to and from whom to expect a curtsey. The wedding of Nicholas Soames in May 1981, provided a welcome change (above).

(Previous pages) Both the Queen Mother and her eldest daughter are keen racehorse owners. Ascot lies within the sphere of the Queen as an owner as she is more interested in the Flat. The Queen Mother, on the other hand, prefers steeplechasing. One of the most successful owners in the country, the pinnacle and nadir of her career came in 1956. In that year she entered her horse Devon Loch in the Grand National. With the final fence behind him, Devon Loch was well out in front when his legs collapsed and the Queen Mother's chances of winning the Grand National were gone. In her more ordinary round of engagements (these pages) she has always continued to appear happy and confident no matter how disappointing the events of her private life.

Margaret's wedding some thirteen years later. The dazzling diamond and ruby tiara, worn by the Queen Mother (these pages), was produced from the Queen's own private collection of jewels. (Overleaf) The Queen Mother with her family and the Duke of Beaufort at the Badminton Horse trials.

The Queen Mother's magnificent collection of jewellery is justly famed. For her wedding in 1947 Princess Elizabeth borrowed a tiara from her mother, the same tiara was again used at Princess

(Previous pages) Special cheers greeted the Queen Mother at the wedding of her grandson and Lady Diana Spencer in July 1981. (Facing page) The Princess of Wales accompanied the Queen Mother to the annual Braemar Games in 1982. This was the Princess' second appearance at the Games that the Royal Family have attended for the past sixty years.

(Previous page) Many members of the Royal Family turned out for Ascot in 1983. The Queen, Princess Anne and the Queen Mother were all prominent, as were the Gloucesters (bottom left). Other members of the family have accompanied the Queen Mother to various equestrian events. (Facing page, top right) Princess Michael of Kent at Epsom 1982, (bottom right) with the Queen at Epsom, (top left) with the Queen again in 1982, (this page below) with the Queen, Prince Charles and Princess Anne at Ascot. The Trooping the Colour Ceremony (overleaf in 1983), held every year on the second Saturday of June, the Sovereign's official birthday, is one of the great ceremonial occasions of the year. Hundreds of troops, in full dress uniform, parade before the Queen in a traditional ceremony dating back to the days when the colour was the regiments rallying point amid the smoke and confusion of battle. After the trooping the crowds gather around the Victoria Monument for a glimpse of the Royal Family on the balcony of Buckingham Palace.

(Previous pages) the Queen Mother's ready smile endeared her to thousands when she first entered the Royal limelight following her marriage to the Duke of York in 1923. The early Empire Tour of Australia confirmed the popularity of the new Duchess, and of the Royal Family. Throughout that tour and her subsequent public life the Queen Mother has always allowed a genuine warmth to shine through. Sometimes it is in the form of a gentle smile and at other times an ebullient enjoyment of the occasion brightens everything.

Since the untimely death of her husband in 1952, Queen Elizabeth the Queen Mother has continued to fulfil the task and duty that she took upon herself in 1923. Her new role has been to become 'Granny to the nation,' earning for herself the recognition of being the best loved member of the Royal Family.

Frilled, Chinese, crossover and wing collars – the Princess of Wales' neck lines are often the details which give an otherwise ordinary dress chic. Not that the crowds bothered too much about such minutiae – they just loved Diana. 'She's GORGEOUS' was the cry Down Under, and in Canada, 'Those lovely eyes.'

You could say fashion went straight to the Princess of Wales' head – her hats, all designed by John Boyd of Knightsbridge – set a new craze for headwear. And that despite the fact that the Princess of Wales sometimes wears her hats the wrong way round – back to front or even sideways; the hats often look better for it. The Princess' first major hat event came at her first Ascot – and she passed with flying colours in a veiled pill box, a red boater and an ostrich feather hat. The Prince of Wales likes to see the Princess wearing hats with little veils which only just cover her eyes. The misty effect they give certainly highlights the Princess' stunning, wide blue eyes. One glance from them can make strong men crumble!

It didn't seem possible that the blushing young Sloane Ranger could transform her ultra-relaxed Sloane style – a mix of pin-striped skirts, lacy tops, baggy cotton print skirts, loose shirts and oversized pullovers – to a fashionable Royal elegance in two short years. But the Princess took her new job seriously, worked hard at her model girl looks and chose clothes which put her at the centre of the fashion world. Exercise and diet changed the Princess from a pretty young bachelor girl to a beautiful young woman. On tour she took her hairdresser, but no make up artist – nature gave the Princess all she needs.

Now and then the Princess abandoned demure pastel or primary colour blocks, pretty prints and discreet flower patterns in favour of stripes. Bold stripes, broad stripes . . . beautiful stripes. In Ottawa when the Princess wore the silk striped dress (above) she had already captured the heart of a man who knows more than enough about beautiful women – Canada's leader Pierre Trudeau, pictured behind the Princess. But for an Australian Church service two months earlier the Princess of Wales' stripes (left) were less flamboyant.

Touring with the Princess of Wales is like touring with a flower shop. No sooner does her official car stop than children rush forward to press posies into her arms. Every bunch, from large bunches of bought flowers, to tired-looking wild flowers little children pick in the countryside, are passed by the Princess to her Lady in Waiting or to policewomen. No sooner has the Princess accepted a few bunches and passed them back than more flowers are being presented, and sometimes even thrown by the excited crowds. As long as the flower givers put their names and addresses on their gift – no matter how small – they get a letter of thanks from the Princess' household.

Tiaras, said some, would be a problem – how could the Princess possibly wear a tiara with her 1980s hair style? Hairdresser Kevin Shanley proved it was no problem. As the pictures show, the Spencer Family tiara and the Queen Mary tiara look as if they were made for the Princess.

Come rain or shine the Princess had to look her best on tour and trunks were packed with everything from skimpy silk dresses to thick coats. On Ayers Rock the Princess wore a simple, crisp cotton dress by Benny Ong. It looked enviably cool but on the way down Ayers Rock it blew open revealing a slim Royal knee. The photographers below were delighted – the Princess wasn't so happy.

The eyes have it. In Australia many were worried that the meeting between the Royal couple and the newly-elected Republican leader Bob Hawke would be an awkward one. But the meeting went well, and when the Royals left Bob Hawke could only agree wholeheartedly with his wife that the Princess has beautiful eyes.

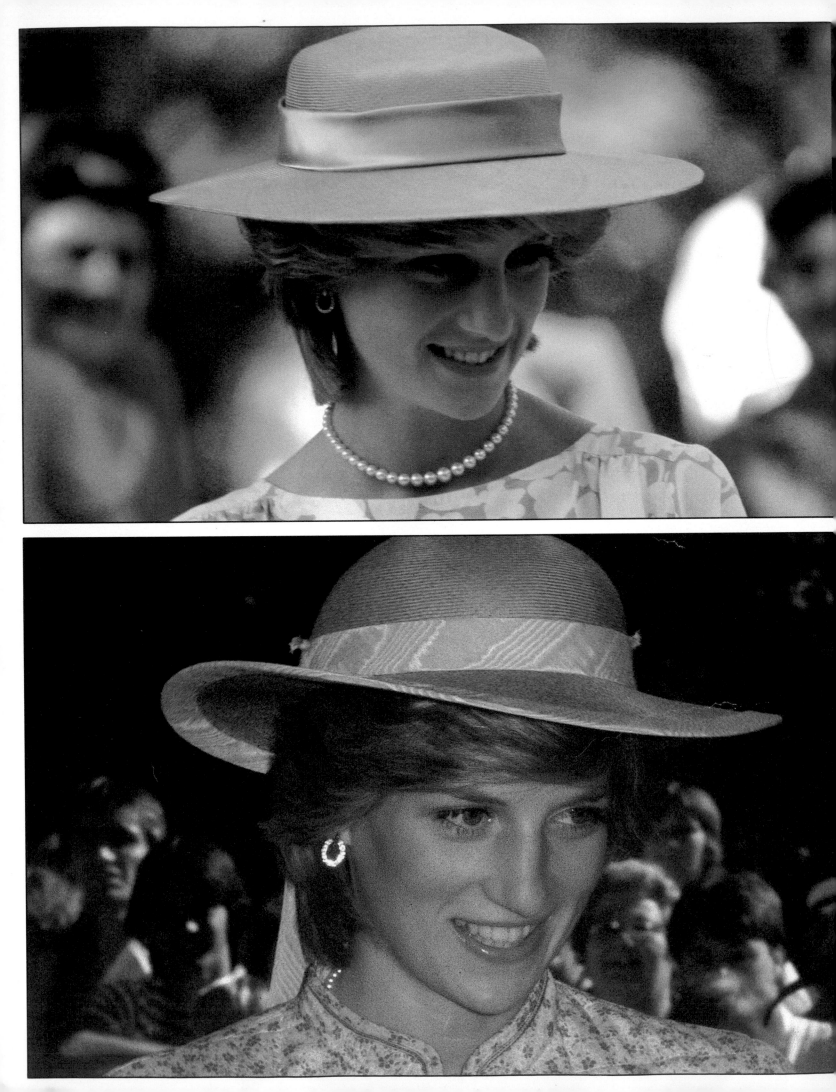

The red dress pictured here was originally made for the Princess to wear at Ascot – two years later the Princess wore it on tour in Australia.

If mum could do it so could the young Prince William! And on two of his earliest press calls the baby Prince showed that his wardrobe was as stylish as the Princess of Wales'. On the journey from his home from home in Australia, the sheep station Woomargama in New South Wales, to Melbourne, William sported the blue and white romper.

Clutching a Canadian flag, the Princess of Wales stayed loyal to British designers. Jasper Conran, Caroline Charles and Donald Campbell are among her favourites. But it will be another year before the Princess of Wales starts giving out her Royal warrants – and until then Buckingham Palace refuse to give out any information about her designers.

The black and white skirt and top by Jan Vanvelden was dubbed 'Di's disco number' when she gave it its first airing at an Adelaide student dance. It came as a surprise to see the Princess in the same clothes at the Governor General's sedate garden party in New Zealand.

Red and white was, appropriately, a colour theme for the Princess in Canada. The white hat trimmed with red (pictured here) went with two red and white outfits. Pillar box red suits the Princess and she wears it often in the day and during the evening. But most colours from pastel shades, through startling primary colours to black look good on the Princess. Orange is one of the few colours she does not wear.

A hint of leg silhouetted through Jasper Conran's demure grey and white silk suit must have delighted the Prince of Wales. He loved the photograph of Lady Diana standing against the sun in a filmy skirt, taken while she was working at the Young England Kindergarten.

Looking Royal on every occasion is no easy task, so the Princess of Wales opts for natural fabrics – like cotton, wool and silk. Her off duty clothes are also natural fibre. The Princess loves unusual knitwear – her Sally Muir black sheep jumper is a favourite.

By day the Princess' fashions sparkle – by night they dazzle. The evening dresses and ballgowns she brought on tour showed how far the Princess' fashion sense had come since the pre-engagement days when her evening dresses were sometimes too revealing. In Sydney at the Wentworth Ball, Australian women had spent small fortunes in an effort to look their best, and arrived in everything from glittering space-age style evening wear to Victorian crinoline ball dresses. But that night, like every night on tour, the Princess' dress – she wore the blue and silver ruffled, by Bruce Oldfield – stole the show.

George VI gave aquamarines to the Queen Mother 'to match the sparkle of her eyes'. Today history seems to be repeating itself – the Princess of Wales has been showered with sapphires – the first was her diamond and sapphire engagement ring.

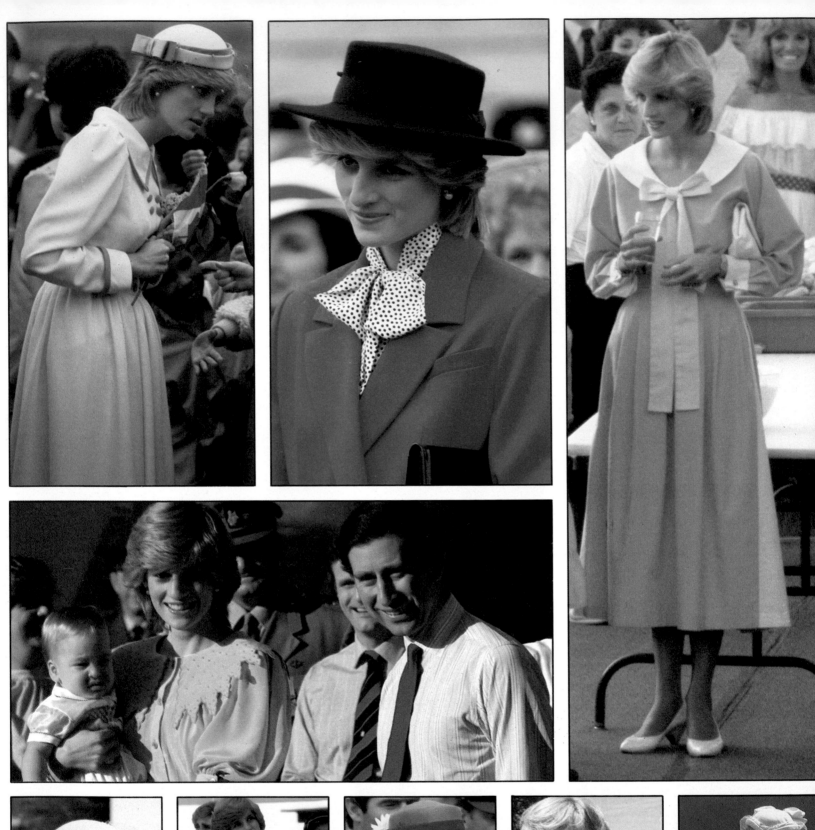

Remember that chic white suit the Princess of Wales wore in Tasmania? Here it is again but with a huge clown collar to give it a completely new look in New Brunswick, Canada. Canada or Down Under the suit was a hit – especially that coy little slit in the skirt.

Hats are fun as the Princess of Wales has shown, but she decided to go hatless on the last minute, informal tour of Victoria's bush fire area. Earlier on Ayers Rock, when she went bare headed in the blazing heat, some Aussies said she would have been better off with a hat.

In bustle, bows, lace and frills the Princess of Wales looked delightful – and her Klondike-style costume was set off by the prettiest pair of peach kid lace up boots ever seen in Edmonton, Canada. Later the Princess confessed her boned bodice was rather uncomfortable.

Hachi is the proud designer of a dress which took the fashion world by storm. His slinky, one-shouldered silk evening creation embroidered with crystal beads showed the Princess at her most glamorous. The designer, who has a workshop just off Bond Street, does not like traditional ball dresses – he likes his dresses to show a woman's body to its best advantage.

Everywhere the Princess went on tour she brought happiness and laughter with her. In blistering heat, in cold and in rain the Princess kept smiling.

The Princess' designer wardrobe never stopped her doing the things which might dirty a dress or stain a skirt. If she spotted disabled or old people, or tiny children in the crowd, she would make a bee-line for them and crouch down to talk to them so they could hear her more easily. On tour in Canada when the Princess was given some flowers by a blind boy, she guided his hands over her face and clothes so he could feel the different textures.

Quilted jackets became an all important stand-by for the Princess of Wales in Australia and New Zealand, where the weather was very unpredictable. The floral jacket pictured is part of a suit designed by Miss Antonette. The Princess of Wales bought it off the peg from Harrods in the summer of 1982. Apart from wearing the suit in Melbourne she wore the jacket in New South Wales over the blue-green silk dress first worn at Alice Springs at the start of the tour. When the Princess wore the yellow quilted jacket pictured (above) in Waitangi, New Zealand, she managed to keep it crisp and neat despite the fact that the vast tribal canoe which carried her to Waitangi sprang a small leak just before she boarded.

It was their last evening in Canada, and the night before the Princess' birthday – and in celebration the Princess wore a dazzling new red evening dress to a small farewell dinner. Later she got her first official birthday present – a dressing table set in a deep red box decorated with a large red velvet bow.

Critics said the Princess' dresses were dowdy, middle-aged and, above all, too long. Few could agree with the first two criticisms. As for the latter, there is a practical reason for the Princess of Wales' longer than average dresses. She tends to bend over to talk with children and with people in wheelchairs, or to pick up cards and flowers thrown by eager admirers. By keeping her skirts longer rather than shorter the Princess has found she can avoid embarrassment.

One of the first pieces of jewellery the Princess of Wales made popular was the pearl choker. In the Spencer family jewel collection there is at least one fine, multi-string choker. Now the Princess can boast several pearl chokers in her own jewel collection.

Some of the Princess' fashion consciousness seemed to have worn off on the Prince by the time their first tour came round. Her hairdresser Kevin Shanley got to work on the Prince's hairstyle and swapped his old greased-down style for a bouncy, less formal cut which covered his bald patch and disguised his larger than average ears.

'Working the crowds' was second nature to the Princess of Wales by the time she had spent four weeks touring Australia. In New Zealand she even learned not to blush when admirers asked to kiss her hand or cheek.

Every now and then the Princess shows a romantic choice of colours similar to that of the Queen Mother. The Chelsea Design Company's pink and white fine striped dress is typical – it is just the kind of pastel pink the Queen Mother loves to wear.

At 22 years old the Princess of Wales has managed to acquire the easy confidence of an old campaigner. Her success in the fashion field helped build up that confidence, and the Princess' Royal fashion formula – traditional British frocks with a touch of Di magic like a special neckline, an unusual belt, strikingly bold colour combinations or out-of-the-ordinary cuffs – has been a much needed shot in the arm for the British fashion industry.

Princess Margaret, the Queen's younger sister has always lived somewhat in the shadow of her elder sister and sovereign. However, she has been given her own round of official duties to perform and has attended most of the affairs of state in recent years.
Opposite page: (top right) at Ascot 1982 and in 1981 (top centre), (top left) a film première in 1981, (centre right) inspecting a guard of honour in Germany 1980, (bottom left) at a performance of Swan Lake at the London Coliseum May 1982, (bottom centre) at a garden party at Lancaster House 1978, (bottom right) at the première of Valentino in 1977. This page: (top right) with Lady Diana Spencer and the Queen Mother at the wedding of Nicholas Soames in May 1981, (centre left) at Ascot 1981, (centre) at the Burlington House Fair in March 1982, (centre right) at the ballet in 1982, (bottom left) with the Queen Mother on the occasion of her eightieth birthday, (bottom centre) at Ascot 1982, (bottom right) during the visit of King Birendra of Nepal.

The Prince and Princess of Wales drove in an open car to celebrate the 650th anniversary of King Edward III's charter to St Columb, in Cornwall. While there Prince Charles received a book about British trees, published in 1906 and dedicated to King Edward VII. (Following pages) the Royal Family on the balcony after the Trooping the Colour Ceremony in June 1983.

The 9th of March 1983 found the Princess of Wales in Devon to launch an appeal for £400,000 for the county's facilities for the under-fives by visiting playgroups in Tavistock and Bovey Tracey. At the Tavistock playgroup (right and below) she joined in a birthday party, singing Happy

Birthday to three-year-old Emma Parkin. Later that year, she visited the Royal Preston Hospital in Lancashire, the tour, predictably, included the children's ward.

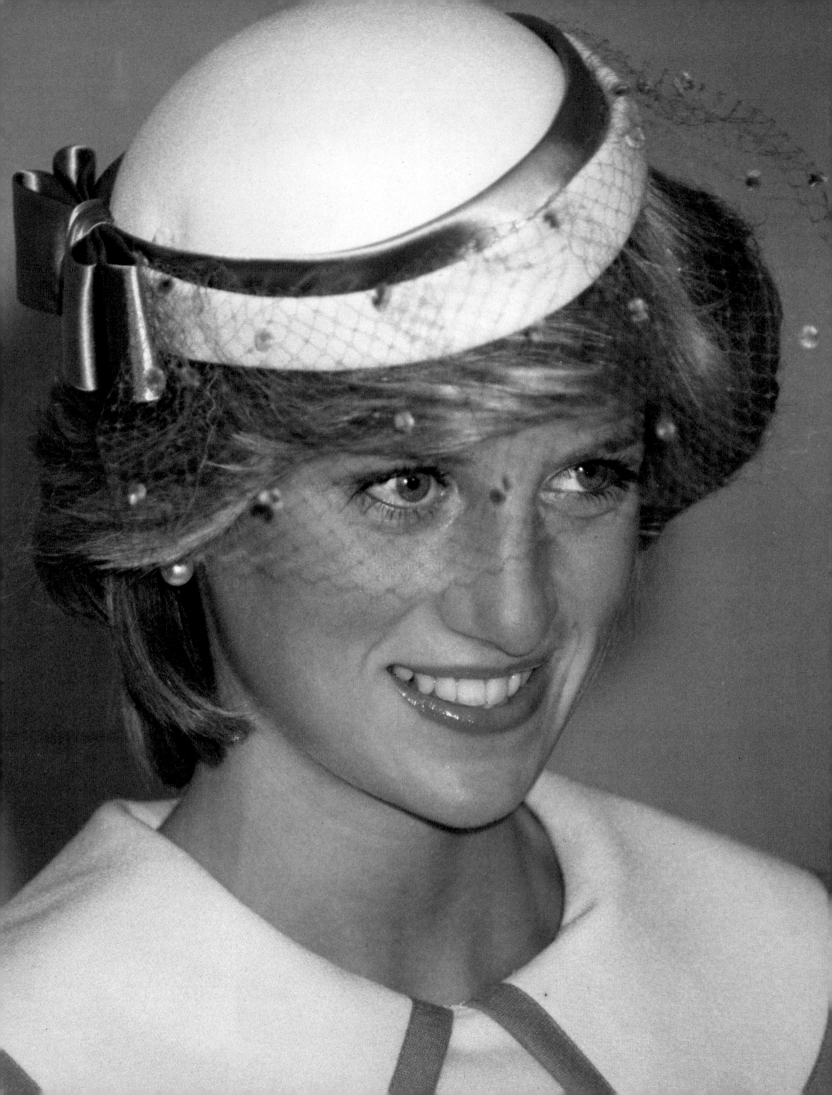

The fantastic reception given to the Princess of Wales during her recent visit to Australasia with her husband seems to have given her added confidence. This was especially obvious at Coberly (this page) and at Canterbury (facing page).

It was a little late for Valentine's Day, but as it was just over two years to the day since her engagement, the Princess of Wales might have thought the heart-shaped bouquet (above) appropriate as she began her visit to Brookfields School for Mentally Handicapped Children at Tilehurst on 25th February. "She's a natural," was the most often repeated compliment. "I'd have her on my staff any day," added the school's headmaster.

On Christmas Day 1982, the Royal Family went to matins in St George's Chapel, Windsor. Prince William, however, was one of four royal infants who were absent. Prince Edward and the Queen Mother could not attend either. Captain Phillips was there (right) with his wife, Princess Anne, and Peter his son. Other royal children present included those of the Kents – Nicholas, Helen and George. Viscount Linley was also there with his sister Sarah.

In recent years Prince Edward, the Queen's youngest child, has been seen more and more often in public. After successfully completing his education at Gordonstoun, where he passed all three 'A' levels and gained an 'S' level, he took up a temporary post as Housemaster at Wanganui, New Zealand. It was here, on April 22nd, that he welcomed his brother and sister-in-law while they were on their tour of Australia and New Zealand. In between times the young prince found time to accompany his family to various occasions.

The Duke and Duchess of Kent have long been among the most popular members of the Royal Family. The Duke is particularly associated with the export drive and the promotion of British technology. He is also the Colonel of the Scots Guards, and it was in this capacity that he helped distribute South Atlantic Medals. His wife is equally well known as a patron of nursing and the arts. The recent illness of the Duchess has caused some concern, especially as she was absent from Wimbledon, but she would appear to be recovering.

Princess Alexandra, who is married to the Hon Angus Ogilvy, is the most junior member of the Royal Family to receive a Civil List Payment. She is renowned for guarding the details of her private life from newspapers and the public, while at the same time fulfilling her public engagements with spirit and enthusiasm. However, it is known that she has been blessed with one of the happiest of Royal marriages. Her husband has managed to steer the difficult path between being considered a parasite, by attending all his wife's functions, and being thought of as disinterested, by attending none. The twentieth anniversary of the Ogilvy's marriage was celebrated quietly in April 1983 and their two children, Marina and James are now on the threshold of adulthood.

Wherever the Duchess of Kent is and whatever type of occasion she is attending, she always manages to appear in fashionable clothes of good taste, which are also in keeping with the spirit of the event. When she and her husband attend functions of state, (top far left) the Opening of Parliament in 1977, there are few that outshine her. On a more serious note, the Duke and Duchess attended the Family Service of Remembrance at Mousehole for the lifeboatmen killed in the Penlee lifeboat disaster (top far right). The Duchess is also a noted music lover, she is a member of the Bach Choir, and in March 1982 she attended a gala concert by the Royal College of Music Orchestra (bottom).

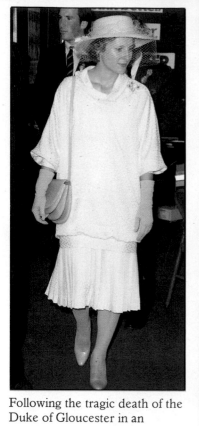

Following the tragic death of the Duke of Gloucester in an aircraft crash, his younger brother, Richard, was raised to the Dukedom. This elevation brought with it a vastly increased work-load. The Duchess, in particular, has been very busy in recent years. Being an accomplished pianist herself, the Duchess is often associated with musical events and organisations.

Prince and Princess Michael of Kent, who have so recently had their marriage recognised by the Pope, do not strictly speaking carry out any official engagements at all. They do not receive money from the Civil List and their activities are not included on the Court Circular. In reality, of course, they carry out some hundred or so engagements a year, most of them to do with sport or the motor industry. The Prince is, in fact, President of the Institute of the Motor Industry and he undertakes over twenty engagements a year in this capacity alone. Indeed, his abiding interest in vintage and veteran cars has prompted him, more than once, to take part in the London-Brighton Run.

"I must retire, with regrets but also with relief, from the many commitments of the past years," wrote Princess Alice, Duchess of Gloucester at the close of her autobiography, published in 1983. For a lady of her age, who has served the Royal cause well for so many years, such a sentiment is not only understandable but long overdue. For many years her staff have marvelled that she could continue to attend so many functions. But her intention to retire was no idle threat and her list of official duties has been dramatically cut to about thirty a year. It is to be hoped that she is as successful in her retirement as she has been in her working life.

Prince Philip has always been interested in sport of all kinds. His abilities as a seaman (facing page top) are, perhaps, not as well known as is his prowess as a driver of a coach and four (this page). He has won numerous trophies at this sport and is a popular and much respected competitor. In 1980, after just seven years at international level, Prince Philip was chosen to captain the British team at the World Championships and he led the team to success. (Facing page bottom) The Crown Prince of Bahrein tries to interest Prince Philip in hawking.

As well as the gala and official engagements which they attend, Prince and Princess Michael of Kent enjoy many sporting events. One of the long term events with which they are involved is the Americas Cup, they gave particular encouragement to the British 1983 entry, *Victory '83*. Wherever they go the Princess manages to look her best.

Throughout his thirty-one years as consort to the Queen, Prince Philip has managed to fill the role admirably. His sense of humour, spirit of adventure and ready wit have become popular hallmarks of the Prince as he travels the world (these pages).

It is only a short walk from Windsor Castle to the venue of the Royal Windsor Horse Show, and the inclusion of Prince Philip among the competitors (facing page) was reason enough for the Queen and Princess Anne and her two children Peter and Zara (this page) to be there – at least for the weekend sessions. Prince Philip entered for the Carriage Driving Grand Prix, which he won in 1982. His eldest son, however, prefers polo (overleaf).

heir apparent to the British
one, Prince Charles has been
iged to join the services of
ich he will one day be
mmander-in-Chief. His
eer in the Royal Navy came
a climax in 1975 when he was
t in command of the
nesweeper HMS Bronington.
ring November 1976 he and
ship took part in an exercise
he Firth of Forth.
fortunately this promising
eer was cut short when his
ies as Prince of Wales took
ecedence. His younger
ther Andrew, however, has
n able to pursue his career
a helicopter pilot in the Fleet
Arm, even to the point of
ing part in the Falklands
r.

Prince Charles is now undertaking a much more varied and busier official schedule than ever before, together with many private sporting events. One of the latter which he seems to particularly enjoy is the annual shooting match between the House of Commons and the House of Lords, (above right) in 1980.

The many honours which belong to Prince Charles bring their own obligations. As Colonel of the Welsh Guards he went to Carmarthen in April 1982 to receive the freedom of the city on behalf of his regiment (far left top and far left centre, left and below centre and facing page).

Prince Andrew's recent adventures, particularly his involvement in the Falklands War, from which he returned in September 1982, and the various rumours concerning his girlfriends, have ensured great publicity and popularity. Though he is determined to continue in the Fleet Air Arm, the new public interest may result in an increased number of engagements.

For many years Prince Charles has been a well-known and competent polo player. His Maple Leaf Team, has won several trophies in recent years, many of them due to the Prince's abilities. However his riding skills have not saved him from the occasional tumble on the field. It is on the polo field that Prince Charles is often seen at his most relaxed, thinking nothing of changing shirts in public (facing page top) nor of slipping behind a hedge to answer the call of nature (below).

The return of HMS Invincible, together with her most distinguished crew member, was a splendid occasion with bands playing and a fly-past. Prince Andrew admitted feeling 'different' after experiencing war at first hand. "When you are down on the deck, when there are missiles flying around, then at that precise moment you are on your own and that's all there is," he commented.

During his visit to Rio de Janeiro in 1978, Prince Charles threw himself wholeheartedly into the spirit of the festivities (facing page). He must have been more than glad to cool off on the Town Hall balcony afterwards (this page, centre left). His first official engagement with Lady Diana Spencer, in the spring of 1982, was no less newsworthy, but not for anything the Prince did. When Lady Diana stepped from the Rolls Royce the crowd of two hundred was reported to gasp simultaneously at her dress. The black evening gown was strapless and had a daring neckline. Despite the dress, and the gathering of notables, Lady Diana seemed both calm and relaxed on her first official outing as the fiance'e of the Prince of Wales.

Princess Anne is not usually thought of as having a direct link with the military, but she is Colonel-in-chief of three regiments. These appointments involve her in many duties, especially visits to her regiments at home and abroad. (Top left) Princess Anne inspecting a guard of honour in 1971, while (above and below right) she attended a passing out parade at Sandhurst in 1973. In 1969 she visited the 14th/20th Kings Hussars in Germany and inspected their modern war machines. She saw the more traditional Hussar uniform when she visited the Kings Troop Royal Horse Artillery November 1982 (below).

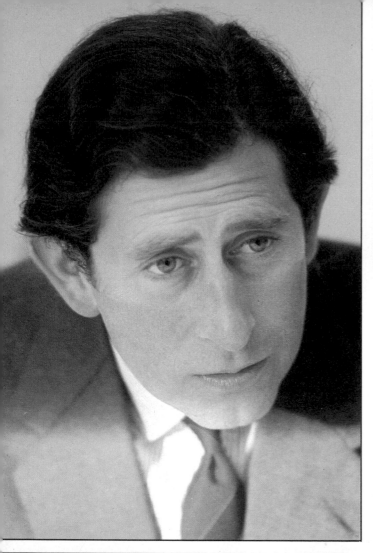

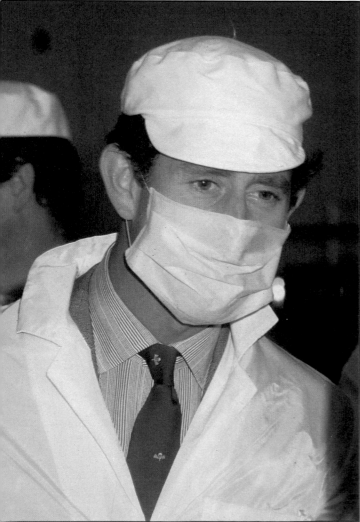

At his many official visits and functions Prince Charles has had to wear a bewildering variety of costumes. Along with the often seen military uniforms, he has worn a garland of flowers on his visit to Mother Teresa's Calcutta Mission (right) and a straw hat to enter the Jama Msjid Mosque in Delhi (above right). Back in Britain, he donned white overalls and a mask to enter the White Room at Brynmawr (far left). This was not for any religious reasons but because the high technology plant demands a dust free atmosphere.

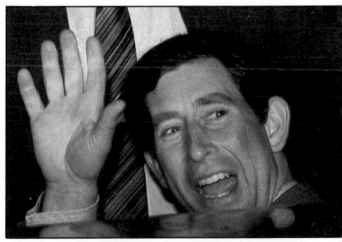

Though the last reigning monarch to lead his troops into battle was George II at Dettingen in 1743, the royal family continues its age-old association with the armed forces, as the pictures on these pages clearly show.